COLLEGE OF ALAM

D0884021

# WITHDRAWN

Gray, Jesse Glenn
   On understanding
violence philosophically
and other essays

## DATE DUE

| MAY 31 '78 | | | |
|---|---|---|---|
| MAY 16 78 | | | |
| MAR 16 7 | | | |
| MAY 4. | | | |
| APR 27 '85 | | | |
| JUN 13 84 | | | |
| OCT 14 '92 | | | |
| JUN 17 93 | | | |
| OCT 27 '93 | | | |
| | | | |
| | | | |
| | | | |

*On Understanding Violence*
*Philosophically*
*and Other Essays*

*J. Glenn Gray*

# On Understanding Violence Philosophically
## Philosophically
### and Other Essays

A TORCHBOOK LIBRARY EDITION
*Harper & Row, Publishers*
*New York, Evanston, and London*

# Contents

To
Martin  Heidegger
in
grateful acknowledgment

# Understanding Violence Philosophically

One of the baffling aspects of our species is its continuing attraction to violence. Though we admit it reluctantly and many persons genuinely dislike to participate in violent scenes, few of us indeed are immune to its inherent fascination.

The Second World War first made me keenly aware of the appeals of violence. I tried in my book *The Warriors: Reflections on Men in Battle* to describe them phenomenologically. The combat soldier as *Homo furens* responds, as I put it in the second chapter, to the lust of the eye, the yearning for comradeship in danger, and the delight in destruction on a massive scale. Though as a cryptopacifist I myself could rarely participate in these appeals, I felt their presence in other soldiers, and my book was a painful effort at understanding such obscure forces in my fellows.

Of late years, with the riots in our cities now spreading to our campuses and becoming a worldwide phenomenon, I have begun to wonder whether man as warrior is an appearance as distinct and isolated as I believed ten years ago. Perhaps the organized violence of war, with its uniformed soldiers, its impersonal weapons, and its rigorous suppression of individual accountability is not as different from civilian life as I then thought it was. Accordingly, and again contrary to my instinctive preferences of subject matter for reflection, I feel compelled to think about violence as a civilian phenomenon—that is, in a wider context than I did in *The Warriors*.

## I

When one looks into the literature on the subject, he discovers soon that philosophers in our tradition have been laggard. Unfortunately they have written little about violence as such. On the other hand, there is a great deal on political and military violence by historians, the psychologists have written about violence, and lately anthropologists and biologists have been publishing books on the subject.

I have read a good deal in the recent scientific literature on aggression and group territorialism of various animals. The current dispute appears to be whether aggression, often alleged to be the cause of violent behavior in man as well as monkeys, is innate or acquired in society. This attempt to apply observations drawn from animal behavior to human violence by men like Konrad

Lorenz, Anthony Storr, and many others is not convincing to me. I am not inclined to treat their observations with the sunny sarcasm of Hannah Arendt, who writes:

In order to know that people will fight for their homeland we hardly had to discover instincts of "group territorialism" in ants, rats, and apes; and in order to learn that overcrowding results in irritation and aggressiveness, we hardly needed to experiment with rats: One day spent in the slums of any big city should have sufficed. I am surprised and often delighted to see that some animals behave like men; I cannot see how this could either justify or condemn human behavior.[1]

To me there is a mysterious chasm lying between man and other species on our planet, which neither scientists nor philosophers have yet succeeded in explaining. I grew up on a farm and was early accustomed to taking care of domesticated animals without sentimentality and to killing wild game in the autumn. Yet the absence of sentimentality in learning to take care of animals can instill a certain attachment, properly called sentiment. The "sport" of hunting I gave up rather soon after watching a creature I had wounded squeal in painful death throes. Later as a soldier I was frequently struck with horror by the spectacle of suffering we inflicted on these innocent creatures who were caught accidentally in frontal areas. After the war was over and slaughter ceased, I remember still vividly braking my jeep to a halt while driving through a German forest to watch two American soldiers casually shoot an antelope on a distant hillside, then climb back into their vehicle and drive off.
From such experiences I have become profoundly con-

1. "Reflections on Violence," *Journal of International Affairs*, vol. 23, no. 1 (1969), pp. 22, 23. In this and the succeeding section I have borrowed extensively from this excellent essay, particularly her analysis of action and its frustration today.

vinced that man is never on the level of animals. Either he falls below them, as so often in his mad rages, or rises above them when he achieves humanity. Though I never feel inclined to argue about this matter, it gives me a certain satisfaction to hear from veterans of more recent wars that they have come to the same conclusion as a result of like experiences.

This intuition of the incommensurability of man and animal is hardly new, to be sure. I find in Aristotle's ethics the statement that "the incontinent man can do ten thousand times as much evil as the beast."[2] Those who are aware how rarely the sober Aristotle exaggerates will also realize that with our contemporary instruments of destruction, totally foreign to the untechnological Greeks, his remark is seen to be an understatement. The simple point, however, that I want to make is that we are probably on the wrong track in trying to understand human violence from the standpoint of animal behavior.

The underlying and unexamined assumption of so many of our scientists is that man is a rational animal, that is, an animal first of all with the attribute of reason added to him from without, as it were. In being violent he loses this attribute and becomes a beast, that is, irrational. I have gradually become convinced that this philosophical definition of man as an *animal rationale* is inadequate and therefore misleading. Naturally there is something "correct" about it but it is far from "right." By accepting it as a presupposition of our thinking about violence, we go wrong philosophically and get a false start on the endeavor to understand the source of violence within us. In a short essay I cannot, of course, give all my reasons for believing this Western definition of man to be in error. Let me, however, indicate a few of them simply

2. *Nicomachean Ethics*, 1103b.

in outline form. They are drawn in part, as readers will recognize, from my study of German phenomenology and existentialism.

Man is a being who possesses memory, and memory is a large and pervasive component of what we call our minds, as even the common etymology of the two words indicates. In Greek mythology, Mnemosyne, goddess of memory, was a titaness and mother of the Muses of Zeus. Even slight reflection is sufficient to convince us that reflection itself inseparably belongs to memory. Recollection is the collecting of ourselves, the gathering of what we have been and still are as well as what we expect to become. Recollection is able to cut across clock time in such a fashion that the near becomes distant and the distant near. This collecting *in* memory and *of* memory can transmute everything so that a seemingly trivial new experience changes the whole of one's perspective on one's past. More dramatically, the recollection of a forgotten incident in childhood may alter radically one's present and future relations to oneself and one's fellows.

Who of us has not been haunted by the recall of a momentary act of violence in himself or his companions, an act or even a gesture sufficient to propel us from the periphery of an angry mob toward its center? Similarly, there is hardly a violent man who on occasion has not been moved by an act of tenderness that will not cease to trouble him till his death. The intensity of memory bears frequently little relation to the duration or importance of what it recollects. Normal connections of cause and effect seem curiously out of balance here, indeed hard to discover at all in many instances. Memory makes self-knowledge difficult to the point of impossibility, for the self is not only ever in the making but is subject to no discoverable laws of orderly progression.

Hence memory is an uncanny but wonderful part of

being human. Only to the thoughtless is it simply a
faculty of recalling what has been.[3] Animals, too, have
memory in this limited sense of recalling the factual past.
But presumably they do not inhabit their memories;
memory for them does not transform past, present, and
future as it does for us. They are not made "mindful"
enough by memory to speak in tongues, to become guilty,
or to make their existence in time a problem.

Men also possess imagination, and this power involves
more than the reproduction of past images. It signifies
also productive capacity. Imagination opens up to us the
vast realm of the possible, which is a world more com-
modious than any actual world. Imagination enables us
to live outside ourselves in space as memory enables us
to live outside the present in time. Both, however, permit
the gathering of the distant in the near, the bringing into
presence of that which has been as well as that which
never was.

Shakespeare understood so well this double nature of
imagination as productive and reproductive, as the intricate joining and harmonizing of the real and the
possible:

> And as imagination bodies forth
> The forms of things unknown, the poet's pen
> Turns them to shapes and gives to airy nothing
> A local habitation and a name.

Surely man becomes human in any authentic sense
only when this twofold power of imagination is made
use of by him to create the poetry, painting, and music

3. Martin Heidegger, *What Is Called Thinking?*, trans. Fred D.
Wieck and J. Glenn Gray (New York: Harper & Row, 1968). See
Part II, Lectures III and IV, for a provocative treatment of
memory.

of a people as well as their scientific discoveries and philosophies. This second nature into which a youngster is gradually transformed, if he is fortunate, is much more decisive than the accident of his biological first nature, for it allows him the possibility of giving in his turn a local habitation and a name to what would otherwise remain a chilling and lonely expanse of world.

Such a capacity of imagination, when reflected upon, never ceases to excite our wonder—even astonishment, a sentiment Aristotle saw as the origin of philosophy as well as of art and science. His teacher, Plato, called these powers *ekstasis*, which is the ability man possesses to transcend his specific situation, to get outside himself in space and time. They permit him to participate in others' experiences, to understand what women go through in having a baby, if we are males, or to understand what men go through in mortal combat, if we are females. So often the traditional conception of man as a rational animal misses this dimension of *ekstasis*. It tends to conceive imagination as simply reproductive in the same way it conceives memory only as recall. The other species may well possess imagination in the limited sense as many do possess the popular notion of memory. But the capacity of self-surpassing, of bringing into presence, of naming, of ecstatic union of the possible and the actual—this capacity seems to be reserved to human beings.

In intimate association with memory and imagination, though subtly constituting another dimension of being human, man possesses consciousness and conscience. The words *consciousness* and *conscience* do not sound alike accidentally; originally they were the same, signifying "joint knowledge" or "knowing with others." In our Anglo-Saxon tradition, however, conscience has come to be associated with a moral faculty which enables individuals to know right from wrong, good from evil. And consciousness on the European continent, particularly in German philosophy, has been developed as a continuation of the classic Greek understanding of *nous,* or mind in the sense of that which pervades the cosmos and is simply illustrated in man, not alone embodied in his rational faculties. Neither tradition has seen sufficiently, I believe, the unitary character of conscience and consciousness, by which we are at once distinctive individuals and members of the human community. Both are activities of the productive imagination and memory by which we are placed in the midst of the world and are inseparable from it by virtue of our ability to know jointly with our fellows. Consciousness and conscience allow a participation which makes man distinctive to a greater degree than either memory or imagination can when considered in separation.

Conscience is usually thought of psychologically as an inner state of the self. Conscience makes us guilty, we say, when we become conscious of an act of ours (or failure to act) that does not comport with that which memory and imagination have made possible for us. But guiltiness is thought of too superficially if it is understood in ethical terms alone. We awake to guilt when we first become self-conscious. Without sufficient consciousness or awareness we are unlikely ever to feel guilty, and without responding to guilt, that is, becoming responsible, we block any growth in consciousness of our being with others. It has become usual to understand conscience not as some divine imperative within but simply as the internalizing of the mores of our particular culture. While this is doubtless true, its significance is both different and greater than often believed. Conscience is "social" as consciousness likewise is in the sense that neither would come to be in isolated creatures. The new dimension they bring to the fore is the ontological priority of the communal and community as the fount and origin of all memory and imagination in individuals.

We are gradually relearning today what the ancients already knew, that language is the common possession making man human. Though languages are relative to particular societies, language itself is not. And it is language which forms and largely determines all of us from birth. Consciousness seems to be a linguistic phenomenon, and this phenomenon is the source of all our *joined* knowing and caring and creating in the arts and sciences and in everyday living. Language is much more than logic, as it is certainly other than a tool of communication. It would be more in line with the actual situation to say, as Martin Heidegger has remarked, that our communication and our logic are the instruments of language. In any event, it appears clear that consciousness and conscience as the new dimension formed by and united with memory and imagination are the consequence of that inexhaustible public reservoir called language, which we still so imperfectly understand.

To develop any of these three ideas in detail would certainly require a book-length study and carry me away from the limited purpose of an essay on violence. I mention them in such sketchy and preliminary fashion only to indicate the limitations of the dominant notion that man is adequately characterized as an animal with reason, an attribute which he loses when he behaves violently. There are assuredly more aspects of the human situation that distinguish us from the other species and they from us. I am not inclined to believe that these distinctions make us superior to the animals in any moral or even ontological sense. What I am alone insisting on is the difference, a difference of kind rather than of degree.

## II

The appeal of violence, perhaps especially for the younger generation today, results from the increasing difficulty of acting effectively as distinguished from mere behaving or reacting. One of the distinctive features of being human—when we put aside the definition of man as *animal rationale*—is the achieving of individuality through meaningful action. It has long seemed to me that the definition of freedom as the power to act is the soundest and most comprehensive way of understanding this important but ambiguous quality of human existence. To be sure, this presupposes that we think of action as something more and other than mere physical doing. We act when we speak with authority—that is, reflectively—and a statesman's speech can be frequently more truly an example of action than an inconclusive battle which costs many lives. Or at a less exalted level, a person acts when he takes charge of himself by resolving to choose his own course on a particular issue and no longer to follow unthinkingly the directives of his family, his school, his firm, or even his government. Action is always, as I see it, an assertion of one's individuality, hence of one's freedom, against the manifold forces playing upon us from outside ourselves. Individuality need not manifest itself in defiance of those forces, but it involves a consciousness that they are no longer solely determinative of one's course. There are, to be sure, degrees of freedom as there are degrees of power; neither is by nature absolute. Nor do any of us act very frequently in a full sense, and some people, I suspect, never act at all. Nevertheless, freedom is made actual as distinguished from being simply potential to the extent to which we act and live according to the convictions we have formulated of what is distinctive in us as human beings, either individually or as communities.

As a result of many well-known forces today, such as increasing anonymity caused by industrialization, technology, and overpopulation, it has become vastly more difficult for any of us to act in significant ways or to believe in the importance of our individuality.

What does the frustration of this power to act do to us? The answer seems clear: it creates passions. Passion used to be understood in our tradition as the very opposite of action, a usage that I think we should revive because it is vitally needed. Passion, as philosophers like Spinoza understood, is an undergoing, a being acted upon from without in contrast to an action which is initiated within. As such it is the clearest contradiction of freedom. We still use the word passion in this sense when we speak of crimes of passion and consider passion as an exculpation of the offender because he is not in control of himself. In addition to this primary character of being acted upon, passion also implies that in its grip one suffers. The passion of Christ meant his agonies before and during the Crucifixion. Passion, therefore, in its original and still lingering meaning is a kind of suffering in which we are handed over to external forces, are acted upon, and are rendered unfree.[4]

4. By reverting to this original meaning of the word "passion," I do not intend to rule out its employment in an utterly different sense today, that used by Kierkegaard, for instance, when he writes that faith is a passion and "passion is the shudder of thought." When passion designates the sort of rapt amazement which thinking may experience at its boundaries, such passion is at the furthest remove from mad rage. As the shudder of thought, passion is indeed akin to what we have been calling *ekstasis* in the poetic, productive sense of the word. Here passion is never separate from thinking, is indeed thought potentiated to its highest degree. For that reason it lacks the negative aspects of suffering, vengefulness, and violence.

The typical response to this passion is violence, usually unplanned and spontaneous. Violence is defined by the *Oxford Universal Dictionary* as "the exercise of physical force so as to inflict injury on or damage to persons or property." As a transitive verb, "to do violence to" is related to "violate." It is important to keep the meaning of the word violence distinct from terms like power, force, strength, and authority. I agree wholeheartedly with Hannah Arendt when she writes, in the essay already cited, that these latter terms refer to different phenomena and that it is a sad commentary on our muddled minds that today they are frequently used as synonymous. A major theme of her essay, incidentally, is that violence and power are more nearly opposites, and that violence is increasing in our time because power is eroding from our governing institutions.

In view of my distinction between action and passion, it may be desirable to discuss briefly the difference between violence and force, as I see them. Whereas most of us can grasp the difference between power and violence, that between force and violence is somewhat more difficult. I find in writers like Georges Sorel and Vilfredo Pareto something less than clarity here.[5] And even the

5. Pareto believes in force as a prerequisite for governing and as "the foundation of all social organization." He decries the use of violence as folly, impractical, and a weakening of the social fabric. "Often enough one observes cases in which individuals and classes which have lost the force to maintain themselves in power make themselves more and more hated because of their outbursts of random violence. The strong man strikes only when it is absolutely necessary, and then nothing stops him. Trajan was strong, not violent; Caligula was violent, not strong." [Vilfredo Pareto, *Sociological Writings*, sel. and intro. S. E. Finer, trans. Denck Mirfin (New York: Frederick A. Praeger, 1966), p. 135.] But later he is capable of damning governments which are not willing "to meet violence with equal violence" in putting down a group of rebellious citizens, and appears to approve the resort to violence

much-read contemporary Frantz Fanon in his *The Wretched of the Earth* seems to be guilty of systematic confusion on this distinction. Though his book has become in our time a kind of bible for those in our country who make a cult of violence, he is occasionally capable of writing about "peaceful violence"[6] and leaving the careful reader in doubt as to what he really means. Indeed, Barbara Deming, who teaches a doctrine of militant nonviolence, can challenge his readers to make the following experiment. "Every time you find the word 'violence' in his pages, substitute for it the phrase 'radical and uncompromising action.' I contend that with the exception of a very few passages this substitution can be made, and that the action he calls for could just as well be nonviolent action."[7] Though Miss Deming makes an eloquent case for nonviolent action and one with which I frequently agree, she does not convince me that Fanon can

---

on the part of private citizens when their government is not willing to use force to curb criminals and rioters.

Sorel is much less ambiguous. He writes that "the term violence should be employed only for acts of revolt; we should say, therefore, that the object of force is to impose a certain social order in which the minority governs, while violence tends to the destruction of that order. The middle class have used force since the beginning of modern times, while the proletariat now reacts against the middle class and the State by violence." [*Reflections on Violence*, trans. T. E. Hulme (B. W. Huebsch, 1912), p. 195.] This is clear enough, and generally Sorel, the radical Syndicalist, approves of violence as the appropriate instrument of the proletariat in wresting power from the ruling classes. But one looks in vain through his book for any sharp distinction of the boundaries separating force from violence. It is hardly sufficient to distinguish them in terms of the classes who may employ one or the other.

6. Frantz Fanon, *The Wretched of the Earth*, pref. Jean-Paul Sartre, trans. Constance Farrington (New York: Grove Press, 1968), p. 81.

7. Barbara Deming, "On Revolution and Equilibrium," *Liberation*, February, 1968, p. 11.

be so interpreted or that he is always clear what he means by the words violence and force.

Force seems to be properly used only in the context of legitimate power and right and as a means to the achievement of communal ends. It may never be exerted beyond the extent necessary to secure these ends, or else it becomes mere violence. At an individual level I may struggle with someone assaulting my wife and daughters and kill him in the attempt to subdue his passion. My act would be justifiable and legitimate. But if I render him helpless and then shoot him in a fit of rage, this is illegitimate violence, even though in a human perspective it would be understandable.

Similarly, a legitimate government may employ all the force necessary to restrain a rioting band of citizens but never "meet violence with equal violence." An illegitimate government may be resisted by its citizens with all forceful means in their power in the name of right and justice, never for the sake of mere destruction or revenge. In short, force is a word deriving from legitimate authority and right; as action it must be based on such authority, either of just laws, or in their absence, on the moral convictions of men in thoughtful association with one another. Violence has no such mandate. As a product of passion, it is the will to triumph through destruction of all opposition.

Externally, of course, force and violence frequently look much alike. A foreigner in any land, if he chanced on a scene of coercion in the streets, might well be unable to distinguish an officer of the law from a thief or a victim of violence from perpetrators of violence— and this quite independently of the fact that officers at times behave violently, contrary to law, and that citizens at times act forcefully, within the law. The distinction I am making is never descriptive in any obvious sense of the term, though it describes philosophically a state of affairs that every community of men seek to bring about when they abandon the condition of savagery. The claims of right and justice as opposed to physical strength and might depend on memory, imagination, and conscience for their validation. From them have arisen our civil laws and governments, always imperfect and relative embodiments of the persisting search for social and political self-realization under law.

The institutions that spring up as a consequence of this search for a civilized condition are exceedingly varied and sometimes impede human freedom. This occasions the bafflement of an outsider in a strange land; he does not participate in the slow evolution of that society's forms and structures, its "second nature," as Hegel would say. Even for the initiated citizen it is difficult enough on any given occasion to be clear about the legitimate and illegitimate use of authority by his state.

Such bafflement is not meliorated by the anarchist who steadfastly denies the possibility of any distinction between legitimate force and illegitimate violence. For him any government, democratic or otherwise, is an encroachment upon individual autonomy. According to the philosophical anarchist, even the most dedicated advocates of nonviolence as an instrument for effecting reform in existing institutions are simply employing violence in another form.[8] Such attempts to erase the boundaries between justice and might are a feature of every epoch. In a time like ours they confuse the many who are outraged by the insolence of office and governmental arbitrariness. But anarchy has rarely gained much support, even among the nonthoughtful majority.

8. See the article "On Violence" by Robert Paul Wolff, who takes the anarchist position, in *The Journal of Philosophy*, vol. 66, no. 19 (Oct. 2, 1969).

There are, to be sure, instances in which the boundaries between force and violence are exceedingly cloudy. In desperate situations, such as concentration camps, violence may be legitimate as the sole means through which the doomed victims may rescue a shred of their integrity before death. If there are men dominated by pure malice, an active principle of evil, there may at times be no recourse left to us but resort to discriminate violence, however incalculable its consequences may be. In warfare between nations, too, the distinction between force and violence quickly breaks down, but that is an issue with which I am not concerned here.

One must not, as Aristotle observed, seek to be precise any further than the nature of the subject matter permits. In the sphere of practical wisdom there is no place for absolute judgments and no sense at all in seeking to lay down absolute rules of conduct. But unless we do clarify the relative difference between force and violence and try to apply it in our lives, thinking and action are surely lamed and even frustrated. I at least find clarity in linking violence closely to passion, whereas force is a quality of action.

Passion, however, is a word too general to characterize the particular source of violence in civilian life of our day. To describe some of these manifestations I think we have to speak of rage, even mad rage, employing the word mad in the sense of devoid of sanity. Rage is in every respect a passion, not an emotion. It has little in common with anger, which frequently is a necessary and desirable emotion leading to action. Rage grips us from without, takes us out of ourselves. It is *ekstasis* in the bad, even evil, sense of the word. We reflect too little on the double nature of the ecastic state of mind. On the one hand, it is a source of man's highest productivity in science, art, and religion. On the other, like most of the finest potentialities, it can be the fount of irredeemable malice. Rage is bent on destruction for the sake of destruction. It echoes always the Mephistophelian cry in the drama *Faust* that "all created things deserve to be destroyed."

As I study the faces of students in my college classes, I am sometimes greatly tempted to warn them that they have not the slightest idea of what they are capable. This rational dialogue we are carrying on together is likely to seem to some of the sheltered ones the dependable face of reality. At moments I, too, can let myself forget that these eager youths, very much centered in the activity of reflection, possess another nature. Yet I need only close my eyes to imagine those faces contorted with hatred, those hands, feminine or masculine, clenched or claw-like, those bodies tensed and ready to spring, in order to realize that all of us conceal, half-knowing, powers that are at the furthest remove from the present setting. More precisely, these powers are not *in* us but fall *upon* us, and render us capable of anything. How does one explain this to those who have never been so seized? The literature we study helps, yet only the most imaginative can get a partially adequate grasp of either the creative or destructive force of *ekstasis* from a college discussion, however intense it may be.

Hitherto our civilization has been shielded against this  rage by its relative powerlessness. The violent man without weapons can create a shambles in his immediate vicinity but is easily subdued by police forces. But with the incredibly potent, miniaturized weapons of our contemporary *Homo faber* he can now destroy not only a neighborhood but a whole city. Who of us can repress a shudder when we dare to reflect deeply on the prospects of revolutionary violence in our age of technology?

And this shudder of dread persists when we meet, as

so frequently today, young people who are so utterly alienated from American culture, perhaps even from Western civilization, that they seem to welcome its destruction. These enraged ones are not simply a criminal element, such as are found in every society, but some of the more brilliant and gifted members of our society. When one finds them in a college class, their presence may be at once upsetting and profoundly enlightening.

It is difficult indeed to understand their mood, their temper of mind and disposition of heart. Yet it is urgently necessary to try and not to rest content with generalizations. What first strikes a superficial observer is the unkemptness of these young men and women. At times they remind one of nothing so much as scenes from a pictorial history of the American Civil War! Their external unkemptness is in itself not important, however annoying it may be to the bourgeoisie. But insofar as it may be a symptom of inner unkemptness it is disquieting.

The most disturbing evidence of an inner neglect is the misuse of language on the part of a militant minority of our well-educated youth. Equally deplorable is the fact that this abuse of language is rapidly spreading to many of their educated older opponents as well. Plato held, rightly, I believe, that "to use words wrongly is not only a fault in itself; it also corrupts the soul." This is a statement that requires more reflection than we usually accord it. I do not refer especially to obscene language, employed by them as a mark of their defiance of accepted standards of decorum. I am much more concerned with vituperative epithets and the contempt for careful and precise distinctions of meaning. It is as though, in their suffering and unhappiness, they were using language as a weapon, analogous to pistols and bombs, without concern either for its flexibility or beauty. In their mouths language becomes a succession of slogans in the original meaning of slogan as a battlecry or warcry. This marks, so I believe, a deterioration of mind and character that is attributable to long-continued indulgence in passion.

There is a virtue in the careful use of our mother tongue that exceeds many other virtues, since it is the use of language that makes us human in the first place. As our common heritage, it is infinitely more worth preserving than nations and specific arts and sciences. If in passion we lose our love and care for our native tongue, we will have lost what can hardly be restored.

We take comfort in the circumstance that these radically alienated militants, young and old, are so few. But there is a much larger group of those unable to act who drift into a passion that is less than rage or fury, which may be called resentment. Perhaps the French word *ressentiment* gets the fuller meaning of this frame of mind or heart, because it retains the notion of sentiment. Resentment is truly a passion, not an emotion, stemming from an inability to act. Resentment can only flail about impotently.

The philosopher Nietzsche understood best this lamentable evil of our species. He emphasized the element of suffering in all resentment and its consequence in the desire for revenge. In *Der Wille zur Macht* he writes, "It is impossible to suffer without wishing to take it out on someone; even every complaint contains revenge."[9] And in *Thus Spoke Zarathustra* he speaks of the resentful ones as tarantulas and warns against all "in whom the impulse to punish is powerful."[10] Later in the same book, he explains why we should distrust the impulse to punish.

---

9. Friedrich Nietzsche, *Der Wille zur Macht* (Leipzig: Gesammelte Werke, 1903–1912), Werke XI, p. 253 (my translation).

10. Friedrich Nietzche, *The Portable Nietzsche*, sel. and trans. Walter Kaufman (New York: The Viking Press, 1954), p. 212.

Verily a great folly dwells in our will; and it has become a curse for everything human that this folly has acquired spirit.

*The spirit of revenge,* my friends, has so far been the subject of man's best reflections; and where there was suffering, one always wanted punishment, too.

For "punishment" is what revenge calls itself; with a hypocritical lie it creates a good conscience for itself.[11]

I fear that resentment is an increasing passion in our time. These quotations from Nietzsche and many others that could be cited help to explain why so many who do not actively engage in destruction take a secret satisfaction in the rage of the small minority. It hardly needs to be added that Nietzsche's insights clarify, too, the unreasoning rage of the opponents of hippies, campus radicals, and dissidents of every kind. Resentment deteriorates character as surely as does rage, if more slowly. It makes us accomplices in destruction and enables us to deny participation in such destruction, even to ourselves. This fact deprives us of any possible purgation, which is conceivably not totally absent even in mad fury. If we do succeed in tearing down the precarious fabric of our civilization, it will assuredly not be alone due to the enraged and furious ones but in still greater degree to the passive spectators of that destruction who are getting revenge for their generalized resentments—resentments which have little to do specifically with the human associations and institutions being torn apart.

There is still another dimension to the present mood of our alienated minority which we should strive to understand as best we can. It is their fierce individualism, an individualism that causes them not only to reject the traditional institutions but to reject also any close coop-

11. *Ibid.,* p. 252.

eration with one another. This facet of their mood contrasts sharply with the extremists of the 1930's, whose faith was in underground organizations and associations of the widest variety. In my reflection and research for this essay I was reminded of a section in Hegel's book *The Phenomenology of Mind* which may be of some help in illuminating their present temper. This section is called "Absolute Freedom and Terror" and is concerned with that stage in the phenomenology of culture, that climate of opinion or *Zeitgeist,* which gave rise to the French Revolution of 1789. Hegel is seeking to understand the spirit of that period between the age of Enlightenment which preceded and the Romantic movement to come. The title of this brief but pregnant section of the *Phenomenology* is significant. "Absolute freedom" is meant by Hegel in the pejorative sense of the individual who abstracts himself from all intermediate institutions as well as the state and society, considering his single will to be identical with universal will. Such an individual consciousness conceives the world of external objects and institutions of culture to have "no other nature than that of self-consciousness itself, or conceives it to be absolutely the concept."[12]

This frame of mind denies the possibility of its being represented by any other individual, just as it regards opposition to itself as unreal. Anyone suspected of being opposed to its abstract universalism is guilty without question. When people of this conviction get into positions of authority, their reign is one of terror. As Hegel expresses it, "This undivided substance of absolute freedom puts itself on the throne of the world, without any power being able to offer effectual resistance."[13] Political

12. G. W. F. Hegel, *The Phenomenology of Mind,* rev. ed., trans. J. B. Baillie (London: George Allen & Unwin, 1949), p. 601.
13. *Ibid.,* p. 601.

rule is not really possible for a mentality of this sort, since it is unable to conceive of anything objective to the self, its own self. Its activity exhausts itself in the rage and fury of destruction; there are no positive achievements nor real deeds. Hegel writes of the product of this spirit in a kind of fascinated horror as follows:

The only work and deed accomplished by universal freedom is therefore death—a death which has no inner scope and fulfillment. For what is negated is the unfulfilled atom of the absolutely free self. It is thus the coldest and most sense-less death of all, with no more significance than cleaving a head of cabbage or swallowing a draught of water.[14]

We need not believe that the mentality and mood which accompanied and to some extent produced the French Revolution will recur. Hegel did not accept the idea that history repeats itself. Nevertheless, there is a spirit of intense individualism abroad in our land that dis-believes so strongly in the principle of representation as to approach anarchy, and this is at least reminiscent of that earlier *Zeitgeist* Hegel is seeking to delineate.

If this mood continues to deepen in our populace it could result in a mad fury of destruction with meaning-less death as an essential consequence of such strife. It is not wise to blind ourselves to this dread possibility. Foolish optimism is at least as inappropriate as pes-simism. Both optimism and pessimism are superficial attitudes which tend to hinder efforts to think through our problems and then to act upon them. They look away from concrete problems and bask in complacent judg-ments about the world in general.

Valuable in Hegel's analysis is the recognition of the intimate interplay between the dominant spirit of a

14. *Ibid.*, p. 605. I have revised the Baillie translation here con-siderably.

period and actual events of history. Actual happenings help to create this spirit or mood, to be sure, something all of us realize. But we are much more reluctant to believe that the mood or spirit can help to bring about the events. I at least find that the notion of a *Zeitgeist* aids my understanding of our present militancy and violence much more than the explanation of mimesis, or imitation, which one can read in every newspaper columnist. For what we are confronted with in our city ghettos and our crowded campuses, to a lesser extent all over the land, is a spirit of alienation from traditional forms and mores by which we have hitherto guided our American course. Moreover, it is a passionately individualistic spirit with little use for organization or collective action, either legal or extralegal, a demand for an absolute "freedom from," in which the atomic individual conceives his will to be universal. This accounts for the relentless dogmatism and certainty of being right of our radicals, young and old. Their spirit is a moralistic one, an uncompromising rejection of any social ethics. It is an absolute morality for the individual self, paradoxical as that may sound. What is right for me is a sacred duty for me. All compromise is denounced as hypocrisy, for our present young generation the worst sin of all.

Though such a sketchy analysis of some dominant aspects of our present violent mood is bound to be one-sided and incomplete, it can perhaps lead to a more philosophical understanding when the lineaments are reflected upon. In our time there is a great disregard for intermediate structures and institutions like family, local community, and professional and fraternal associations. Hegel understood so well their necessity for the achievement of concrete freedom as the power to act, in contrast to an abstract absolute freedom which can only react with violence.

Many a young radical today thinks only in terms of himself and something called "the establishment." The absence of relation to and interaction with intermediate structures of the social whole is a striking aspect of this mood. The fruitlessness of this alienation—not all alienation is fruitless by any means—lies in the inability of the radical to find any concrete structures deemed worthy of his support and loyalty. Understood philosophically, it is a failure of consciousness to discover anything but self-consciousness or to gain a foothold in the objective world. Driven back upon itself, this kind of self-consciousness is likely to fall into destructive fury against that which it is unable to join, or to think itself into, or to make part of itself. The mood is one of disengagement from concrete realities, a beating of the wings of thought against the void.

## III

If I were solely interested in an analysis of the phenomenon of violence, I would stop here and elaborate in more careful detail those things already indicated as the roots of civilian violence in our age. But analysis of the problem of violence, however indispensable, is simply preliminary. It seems that our society will never overcome violence; the issue is one of containing it, in itself a maximally difficult task. And if we are to contain both civilian and military violence we shall have first to understand its sources and then act upon that understanding. In our dark times the appeals of violence are so great that unless we seek to reduce these appeals, there may not be any civilization left to analyze for those of us who prefer analysis. Despite my preference in philosophy for Hegel over his successor Karl Marx, I am sympathetic with Marx's famous observation to the effect that "a number of philosophers have understood the world; the problem is to change it." Therefore, let me turn now to some possible ways of reducing the appeals of violence that are suggested by the foregoing analysis.

Everyone realizes that formal education today has assumed a role unparalleled in previous eras. At the same time we have never been more dissatisfied with the kind and quality of the education we are getting and giving. Our dissatisfaction lies not so much with the transmission of information and even of knowledge as it does with our apparent inability to get below the surface of sense and intellect in order to form the dispositions of our youth. In old-fashioned language the failure is one in education of character. Or in my terminology, it represents a failure to instill in young people the capacity to act in contrast to behaving, or a capacity to discipline their emotions in contrast to indulging their passions. It is difficult to know how much formal schooling can remedy this failure in a time when powerful social pressures militate against individual action and discipline of the emotions. Yet there is a kind of despairing faith that education holds the keys to salvation from our troubles.

For this faith to become less desperate, we must seek to narrow the cleavage between formal schooling and informal education, or between learning in the schools and experience in the wider society. Our school systems will have to bridge this cleavage by conceiving education in a more inclusive and activist, in less bookish and abstract fashion, than we have hitherto done. I have argued elsewhere[15] that we must learn to consider service to our emerging world society as an integral part of formal education. This would compel us to give academic credit for

15. In the final chapter of my book *The Promise of Wisdom* (New York: Lippincott and Co., 1968).

work in the Peace Corps and the various domestic corps as well as requiring a year or more of public service for all our youth, emphatically including women. Properly supervised by educators, this field work can and should be as educational as any comparable time spent in the classroom. Since the need for armies is unfortunately not likely to disappear in our chaotic times, it is incumbent on us to transform the military into more of an educational institution, at the same time making it one option among many for the continuation of activist schooling for the rising generations. If we are to become truly serious about "the educating society," these and similar measures must be taken to integrate schooling into the wider context of contemporary experience.

Basic to all this is the ancient but ever neglected idea of Aristotle that you make a child brave, generous, kind, temperate, and just by providing repeated opportunities for performing brave, generous, kind, temperate, and just deeds and not by giving him lectures on ethics. The basic theme of Aristotle's ethics is the great idea of habit—*hexeis*—or habituation to conduct that is under the rule of the mean. The mean is not some middle path but rather an attunement of the self to its own limits and possibilities in which both excess and defect are avoided. Aristotle taught that every man in his first nature is incontinent—that is, given over to appetites that are unrestrained and self-indulgent. Incontinence is mad passion of whatever sort that misses the mean of man in the community of his fellows. Education is the acquiring of a second nature which brings one into attunement with oneself, with society, and with the world of nature. This education is largely a matter of habituation through early and constant practice in the mean of conduct appropriate to one's individual potentialities and society's proper functioning.

Familiar as this ethical principle of habit is to everyone, it has rarely been heeded or put into practice in the formation of character. Indeed we commonly think of habits nowadays in a psychological sense alone and even give them the derogatory connotation of thoughtless mechanical modes of behavior—behaving as distinguished from acting. I am convinced that if we took this ethical principle seriously, it would make our schools as well as our homes many times more relevant to concrete social life. For this sort of habituating is one thing that can insure us against incontinence and passion—the evil kinds of *ekstasis*—which now threaten the foundations of society.

Intimately related to this Aristotelian principle are the writings of Martin Heidegger that relate to dwelling properly on earth. Because Heidegger's thinking is primarily ontological in intent rather than ethical, no one seems to have noticed the connection.

In its widest philosophic significance, however, the notion of habit is one of learning to inhabit this earth of ours properly. Heidegger's ideas are applicable in our technological era to the problem of living or dwelling in a human fashion. He shows in two or three of his essays, not yet published in English translation,[16] the intimate connection among the activities of building, dwelling, and thinking. According to Heidegger, you can dwell only when you get close to things, whether they be natural or of human fabrication. By getting close to, he means living with them, being attentive to the kind of being they are, learning their nature from within as it were, instead

---

16. I refer to the essays "Bauen Wohnen Denken," ". . . dichterisch wohnet der Mensch," and "Das Ding," in the book *Vorträge und Aufsätze* (Pfullingen: Neske Verlag, 1954). They are soon to appear in the Harper & Row series, in the translation by Albert Hofstadter.

of the more typical technological mentality of appropriating and exploiting them as they can be used for us. We must learn to let things be, says Heidegger, which of course does not mean to ignore them but precisely the opposite, to come close to them in their own nature. Only then can we properly build—"build" understood in its widest connotations: not only houses and workshops, factories and schools, but also poems, scientific theories, and political institutions. Thinking, too, can then be transformed from our traditional conception of logical and calculative reckoning into something more poetic, more concrete, and closer to the realities of daily life. So intimately interwoven with the activities of dwelling and building can thinking become as to be nearly indistinguishable from them.

Though Heidegger would probably repudiate any explicit relevance of his thinking to Aristotle's ethical principle, I find an important connection between habit and inhabiting that goes far beyond the etymological tie. We can learn to live properly—that is, to inhabit the earth—if we develop habits of being close to things and to each other. If we can acquire the habits of dwelling rightly in this global era, even in foreign lands among foreign people, by feeling close to them and attentive to the things they are silent about as well as what they say, we may learn to contain the violence in our natures. The art of dwelling rightly is the art of attunement, as Aristotle clearly saw.

It is now recognized that technology has torn man loose from his roots in his natural context and thus robbed him, temporarily at least, of a source of stability and endurance. To some of us it seems apparent that the estrangement from the things of nature underlies the social and political alienation gripping a portion of our youth. As one observes hippies living in the open air and in the wilds, paying no attention to the proprieties of our culture, it is possible to wonder if they are not learning a new kind of dwelling and building and thinking that is not so remote as it seems from the related principles of habit and habituation. At all events, many seem to be happy and gentle, not violent, and in this sense remote from the angry Students for a Democratic Society, with whom they are frequently confused. The urgent need to gain new relationships in depth to those elements in our environment which perdure is surely close to the core of all efforts to cope with the uncanny phenomenon of violence.

This leads to the final and most inclusive possibility of containing violence. Ten years ago in writing the last chapter of my book *The Warriors* I came upon a thought which I have learned to accept still more than when I first discovered it. "A happy people is a peaceful people." Since I am concerned here with civilian violence, not international conflict, I would put it otherwise now. A happy person will never—or almost never—give way to the destructive passions of rage and resentment. On the other hand, the unhappiness that arises from the frustration of action and consequently thwarted self-realization and deprivation of freedom is nearly bound to be violent. What I then failed to see clearly enough is the extent to which happiness, more concretely understood, can be itself a source of action. I want to develop this point in conclusion.

It is usual for us to think of happiness as a state of mind that results from other causes, such as success, a fortunate marriage, a healthy body, or the esteem of our fellows. At the very least, we are accustomed to think of it as an accompaniment to such fortunate circumstances. It was Aristotle, however, who insisted that happiness is not a state but itself an activity, an insight we likewise tend to disregard in modern times. But perhaps we can go further than Aristotle to suggest that the kind of happiness Spinoza and Nietzsche called joy can also be a source or fount of the harmonious or concordant disposition.

In the third book of his *Ethics* Spinoza goes to great length to establish the idea that the one way to overcome the negative passions of hatred, vengeance, envy, despair, and the like is to replace them with the positive emotions of love, generosity, gladness, and other emotions which arise within us, unlike the passions from outside ourselves. Spinoza considers joy to be "man's passage from a less to a greater perfection," whereas "sorrow is man's passage from a greater to a less perfection."[17] And he was certain that desire, which is man's most basic nature, more specifically the desire to persevere in our own being, directs us toward action and perfection in contrast to passion and dissolution. Joy is for him, in short, a wellspring of action and activity, once we conceive rightly our true situation in the world amidst man and nature. "When the mind contemplates itself and its own power of acting it rejoices, and it rejoices in proportion to the distinctness with which it imagines itself and its power of action."[18] Rejoicing is hence a source of power, aiding understanding of our essential situation and enabling us to persevere in it. Whatever else can be said of Spinoza's vision of living joyfully—and one can object to it as beyond the reach of most people—it was a counsel he practiced himself throughout his life. There breathes in his writings a spirit of serenity and gladness which is in part responsible for their enduring appeal.

Though very different in spirit from Spinoza, Nietzsche

17. Benedict Spinoza, *Spinoza Selections*, ed. John Wild (New York: Scribner's, 1930), *Ethics*, Third Part, p. 267.
18. *Ibid.*, p. 256.

likewise taught the centrality of joy as a pathway to over-coming the ultimate impotence of *ressentiment*. All his life Nietzsche combated the spirit of gravity and "the ugly dwarf," melancholy, and though in his youth he was under the influence of the pessimist Schopenhauer, he worked his way to a life-affirming and joyful wisdom. "Life is a well of joy," he declares in the second part of *Thus Spoke Zarathustra*, and at the end of the book there occurs his celebrated poem, which closes as follows:

> The world is deep,
> Deeper than day had been aware.
> Deep is its woe;
> Joy—deeper yet than agony:
> Woe implores: Go!
> But all joy wants eternity—
> Wants deep, wants deep eternity.[19]

One looks in vain throughout Nietzsche's writings for a sustained argument to the effect that joy is a well-spring of action whereas woe can merely suffer the passions of rage and resentment. Yet it is clear that he, like Spinoza, is profoundly convinced of this fact. Joy is for him "the plus-feeling of power," "a symptom of the feeling of attained power." "In the essence of joy lies the will to More."[20] This more-principle, as he names it, is the very substance of his ill-understood will to power. The deep eternity that joy desires is not to be comprehended as a temporal everlastingness, but rather as an enhancement of the Now, the moment that contains eternity within it. In order to grasp how Nietzsche seeks to unite the Now and the eternal, one would have to explicate his

19. *The Portable Nietzsche*, p. 436.
20. *Der Wille zur Macht*, fragments 699, 688, 695 (my translation).

doctrine of the eternal recurrence of the same, which does not belong here. Sufficient to our purpose is the insight he attained into the generative power of joy in human lives, a power that enabled him to affirm the suffering that wracked his body and mind and even to triumph over it for a period. And this is hardly a private experience of Nietzsche. Most of us have caught glimpses at least of the more-principle, even though we hesitate in our timidity to ascribe to it other than a psychological validity.

Spinoza and Nietzsche were bolder. They did not shrink from claiming for joy an ontological status as an independent force in human life. Each, however, in his own fashion. For Spinoza joy is the impetus necessary for us to perfect our understanding in its striving to see our small lives under the aspect of eternity. For Nietzsche, on the other hand, joy is the impetus of the will in its endeavor to incorporate the overflowing abundance of life's possibilities at every moment. But both discover in that species of happiness we call joy the origin of man's drive to transcend the merely temporal and to transform the normal enmities and weaknesses of our human estate into their opposites.

## IV

In our present mood in America, there may seem little prospect for lessening the appeal of violence through these "remedies" I have briefly outlined. The ideas of reducing the gap between schooling and education, of habituating or attuning our young to "living into" the social and natural environment, and of instilling the conception of joy as an origin of action—taken together, these ideas amount to a near reversal of our usual perspectives on the world. I am quite aware of this, and also of the fact that profounder reflection on my part would bring forth other "solutions" equally difficult to put into practice. I agree with Nietzsche that man's nature is as yet undetermined and that there is much still uncanny about human existence. Our present modes of life, so different from those of previous generations, will doubtless bring to light facets of human nature none of us has learned to anticipate.

Nevertheless, the only quality that is needed in order to counter present and future discouragement is courage. Courage is a laughing virtue, not simply a grim and tenacious enduring. The courageous are not given to self-pity, which is a widespread disease of our time. That courage which is other than physical bravery welcomes reflection on every aspect of existence, the dreadful no less than the wonderful. And contrary to popular notions, reflection can inspire cheerfulness rather than gloom.

The single faith that seems indispensable to a student of philosophy like myself is faith in the power of reflection. We need not expect that our reflections on violence, or any other subject, will greatly alter the course of human life. Yet it is required of us, I believe, to draw any and all phenomena of daily life through the lens of reflection. If we see very dimly, others may help to improve our vision.

Philosophical reflections on violence, as I have remarked, are not very numerous in our Western literature. It is, therefore, time, high time, that we reflect on this problem in our present context in order to seek means of mitigating it. If the social and natural scientists can be practically more effective than we in the short range, philosophers are more likely than they to uncover the roots of violence by renewed reflection on what it means to be a human being.

# Epilogue to the German Edition of The Warriors: Reflections on Men in Battle

LETTER TO EDITOR OF THE GERMAN EDITION,
OCTOBER 14, 1969

You asked me to give my reflections on changes of mood and situation of my countrymen since the completion of this book over ten years ago. Are Americans not experiencing the world in vastly different ways from the way they perceived it in the late fifties? How would I want to alter the concluding chapter, "The Future of War," were I to write it today in the light of our involvement in the Vietnam conflict?

It is sometimes possible to detect in such questions by

German acquaintances an undercurrent of *Schaden-freude*. Implicitly they are saying something like this: "Twenty-five years ago you Americans prided yourselves on your moral superiority. We Germans were then the outcasts, the despised ones who had visited Hitler on the world. Now your people are in an analogous position in Vietnam, viewed at least in the eyes of many as an aggressive and terrorist nation trying to impose its will on a poor people thousands of miles from your shores. It is true that you warned in this book that there was nothing specifically German about the Nazi dictatorship, that 'every nation contains in itself violent criminal forces, waiting only for an opportunity to appear in daylight.' But frankly we wonder if you really believed it. Could you have surmised then that within a few years your country would be in the moral and political quagmire of today? We are curious to learn how you appraise such a dramatic reversal of roles."

The questions deserve answers; the *Schadenfreude* that may underlie them is another matter. Though understandable as a response to the self-righteousness of many Americans in those years, such an emotion reveals the poison of national resentments that obscure true insight. As the more thoughtful Americans never felt anything but grief in the misfortunes of Germany under dictatorship, so I believe that sensitive Germans today give short shrift to feelings of malicious joy in our American time of troubles. Intellectually you must realize that the crimes of National Socialism are made not a shade less black by the circumstance that other peoples have since then made themselves guilty. In the United States we are still far from a police state, and it is fairly certain that civilian resistance will prevent our sinking into one. Nevertheless, it is clear that violent and sinister forces have gained ground among our people since 1959. Such forces are most evident in the riots and disorder of our cities and on our campuses as well as the callousness of our conduct of war abroad. Less evident but equally disquieting is the nascent doubt on the part of our alienated and self-alienated minorities of the relevance and staying power of democratic principles and virtues.

In regard to this concluding chapter, it may interest you to know that similar questions to yours are being put to me of late by fellow Americans. The other day a young professor remarked: "When I first read your last chapter in *The Warriors* I dismissed it as hopelessly idealistic. Now I have changed my point of view. At the moment it seems to me far more realistic, almost a higher kind of common sense. Please tell me why this is so. I don't understand myself any more." Soon after the book appeared in 1959, more sophisticated friends than he praised *The Warriors* in letters and conversation, but often specifically excluded the final chapter from their praise. This fact was a bit painful, I confess, for I was aware in writing the book that the concluding chapter was the one for the sake of which the first six were composed. They were the phenomenological—if you will forgive that forbidding word—preliminaries to the philosophical conclusion of my effort. Though I was far from satisfied with what finally got on paper in that conclusion, I was fully persuaded of the soundness of the ideas presented there.

I would not want to alter these ideas ten years later—and not because some of those who then objected now deny that they were ever in disagreement. To many of us it was evident in the 1950's that to resolve the problem of warfare, international or civil, "a transformation of a deepgoing inner sort will have to come over men." I emphasized that this transformation need not alter drastically the external manner of our lives: it would be

more like "an awakening, a coming to oneself, a discovery of friendship, a falling in love." Such a coming to
ourselves would bring us closer to nature, that word
understood in a simpler, more concrete sense than usual,
sufficient to overcome the "estrangement from what is
most familiar," in Heraclitus' famous phrase.

The remarkable quotation from your German philosopher Friedrich Nietzsche formed the center of that concluding chapter and in some sense is the focus of the
entire book. The idea of a strong people resolving "to
break the sword" and "rather perish than hate and fear
and *twice rather perish than make oneself hated and
feared*" seems to me the very substance of the transformation in the leaders of nations necessary to bring a
decisive change toward a more peaceful world.

You will not be surprised to learn with what anguish—
insofar as I am capable of that emotion—I have watched
the tragic course of our Vietnam War since 1965. Again
and again it has seemed to me that our nation has had
unparalleled opportunities in this conflict to declare to
the world: we made a mistake, we are wrong, we are
going to end this slaughter right now, so far as our troops
are concerned. The effect of a strong nation able to make
such a drastic break with its past might well have been
an electrifying one. To some of us who consider ourselves loyal citizens of the United States, it would have
been an occasion of sober joy. What consequences such
an act might have had on future developments in Vietnam, no one knows. At this point, when many believe
we have effectively lost the war there, such a declaration
would be regarded as a desperate decision. Two or three
years ago it would have been different. I firmly believe it
could have changed the entire international climate. We
might not now be living still, as we have been for decades,

in the shadow of an apocalyptic catastrophe, a third
world war.

Since the required political and moral courage was
wanting, our nation has missed a chance that may not
come again, may never come again. It is not easy for me
to write these words. As one who has chosen his country,
not merely resided here, I have long cherished the hope
that my country might be the one to take the risk—the
dreadful gamble indeed—necessary to reverse the direction of world events. For a superbly strong country like
ours to admit its error and to alter its military course
accordingly needed more resoluteness than our leaders
could summon. Perhaps they should not be blamed, because our people would hardly have understood or ap-
proved. Yet they could have been praised had they dared
such misunderstanding and disapproval for the sake of
a more peaceful tomorrow.

In respect to American leadership, the last decade has
been for us the most tragic of the century thus far. It
began with the quickened hope and nascent inspiration
of John F. Kennedy's Inauguration. Toward the close of
his career there appeared to be a change for the better
in the international climate. Some—including those of us
who were not uncritical admirers of Kennedy's—began
to believe that the world was moving away from the abyss
of nuclear war, if ever so slightly. For this reason his
assassination struck us as potentially the greatest tragedy
of our era. Had he lived, he might have been able to in-
duce our people to take large risks for peace. Certainly
our more thoughtful college youth felt an identification
with his administration that they no longer possess. The
present alienation of these youths from government itself, not to mention its leaders, is probably the decisive
weakness of our present situation. Until that has

changed, the opportunities for bold action are indeed very limited.

Punishment for this failure in courage has not been long delayed. For it is now evident that American technology and manpower have been unable to defeat a small "backward" nation whose soldiers fight with bulldog tenacity and endurance. Men have proved themselves superior to machines; numbers have not prevailed over quality in soldiery. Though I could wish it had happened to another people, I discover a grim satisfaction in this humiliating circumstance. The overweening pride in technology, so evident in our century, requires humbling as a precondition for any enduring peace. From an international perspective few things can be more salutary than the spectacle of a mighty nation, armed with the latest products of its factories and mills, unable to work its will on a tiny, determined people. Most in need of this lesson are our air forces, latest and proudest of our military "services." When the truth comes home to rulers that enemy nations cannot be subjugated simply by remote and abstract destruction from the sky, but only by relentless infantry confrontation on the ground and *underneath* it, then new evaluations of real strength will come into the reckoning, and perhaps increased respect for small nations.

At all events, in Vietnam our pride has suffered a fall, and confidence in military judgments will not be easily restored. Unless we respond to this loss of face by seeking a reckless revenge, the lesson may benefit other powerful nations as well as our own. It has become crystal clear that wars can neither be won nor lost any longer in any meaningful sense of those words. But the intoxication of technological might has hitherto made us reluctant to accept this clear truth. A retrograde mentality has accompanied the most radical metamorphosis in the technology of warfare. I have no way of knowing, of course, how the international situation will have altered when these words reach the printed page. (God grant that the Vietnamese people, north and south, may be less tormented than at present.) Yet there is hardly a chance that the precarious nature of civilization today will be less in jeopardy.

Since the publication of my book, more and more Americans are expressing great concern about the deterioration of our natural habitat. Slowly we are realizing that man can sin against nature. Our technological society is polluting the atmosphere and the rivers and lakes, scarring the forests and countryside, and making life less happy and wholesome. More than ever before, there is a reaction against "the asphalt animal," the city, which has become increasingly uninhabitable. A group of scientists, the ecologists, have found a language in which to remind us of the dependence of man on his natural environment and the urgent necessity of restoring a balance between man and earth. More important, they are speaking philosophically, not as scientists only, much less as technologists. And they are giving an intellectual foundation to the active efforts of the conservationists, who have lately been growing in numbers and strength. These are faint indications—straws in the wind, as they say—that we may be approaching an inner change that will one day make international war intolerable. For I am as firmly convinced as ever that a changed attitude toward our habitat must precede—or at least accompany —a changed attitude toward our fellow man.

The young are as always a source of hope and despair. In contrast to the protesting and violent ones are some who have "dropped out" of the struggle for material success and prestige in middle-class America. During the summers they dwell in great numbers in the out-of-doors,

leading a nomadic existence. Though they dress outland-
ishly and some of them are addicted to drugs, while
others have little regard for private property and other
proprieties, it is not impossible to detect in them a certain gentleness and even joyousness. At times one
wonders if they may not be a new sort of John the
Baptist, who herald a change in our disposition toward
nature. At most they can be no more than a herald, for
few of them have any ambition to "prove" anything—
that is, change the world—by their radical manner of
life. One thing is clear: these dropouts can hardly be
effective conscripts for military service. When a majority
of our youth can no longer even imagine themselves as
soldiers, we will surely be closer to "the great day" which
Nietzsche prophesied.

There remain many ways of moving in the direction
toward "the breaking of the sword." At the moment in our
country there are strong voices demanding an activist
role for intellectuals and academicians. Our university
disciplines, especially in the social sciences, are being
drawn toward participation in practical issues and away
from pursuit of theoretical truth. Some of us, however,
remember the words of the contemporary philosopher
Martin Heidegger: "thinking is an act, and indeed an
act that surpasses all practice." The last clause may well
be an exaggeration, but surely the first one is true.

In seeking the sources of war and peace in human
nature, thinking will frequently shudder and be aghast.
Yet it is this "shudder of thought" that once induced
Kierkegaard to make the leap of faith and thereby deepen
Protestant and Catholic theological life. Doubtless it will
require more than one such shudder to bring to pass the
transformation of man about which I wrote in this book.
Yet if the transformation comes it will be via the agency
of thinking, a thinking then overpowered by reality itself,

in this case the dreadful realization of imminent destruction.

I am happy that others are working for peace in the United Nations, the Peace Corps, and in protest marches and active opposition to the military policies of their governments. Thinking is hardly the only kind of effective action. And activists can also be thinkers, perhaps can only learn the deeper secrets of human nature through such action. At the same time I am more convinced than I was ten years ago that philosophic thinking on the ultimate sources of violence and war can contribute more than a little to the kind of shaking of the foundations and consequent self-recollection that must precede the founding of peace. As a result I am far from apologetic about remaining with my philosophy students and at work in my study. Teaching and writing are for me the most useful activities in the pursuit of peace and despite the darkened skies at present are a source of increasing happiness.

# Splendor
# of the Simple

The title of my essay is taken from a poem Martin
Heidegger wrote in 1947 called "The Experience of Thinking."[1] The poem consists of about a hundred lines with
many of them containing four or five words only, including this one: *Die Pracht des Schlichten*. When one
considers how involved and often obscure most of
Heidegger's writings are, the question is natural: Why
would he write such a phrase? Why is the simple so
splendid? In this paper I want to consider these questions,

1. Martin Heidegger, *Aus der Erfahrung des Denkens* (Pfullingen: Gunther Neske, 1954).

using the poem and his equally brief meditation entitled "The Field Path"[2] as the focus for my reflections.

## I

By the question "Why would he write such a phrase?"
I do not mean the man so much as I do the philosopher
Martin Heidegger, or as he prefers, the thinker. Though
the personality cannot be separated from the thinker,
there are sharp limits to any biographical explanations
taken by themselves. But let me begin with them. When
I first met Heidegger in 1955, I was overwhelmingly impressed by his simplicity. And this first impression re-
mains uppermost in the many times I have seen him
since then in Freiburg and the one time in his home
town of Messkirch. I have walked with him down the
field path he took so often as a boy, viewed the house in
which he grew up beside the St. Martin's Church in which
his father was the sexton, and also worked over manu-
scripts with him in his second study at his brother's home
there, where he continues to write many of his essays.
If it be characteristic of the simple man to remain at-
tached to his birthplace and familiar haunts, Martin
Heidegger's constant returns to Messkirch throughout his
long life lend him this simplicity.

We usually associate simplicity with the meaning of
the artless, the ingenuous and unpretentious, with rural
manners and country people who are close to nature.
Here, too, Heidegger qualifies. Though his writings contain the word "nature" rarely, his philosophy is replete
with the sights and sounds of the region from which he
comes. His philosophy is as truly at home in the woods

2. Martin Heidegger, *Der Feldweg* (Pfullingen: Gunther Neske,
1954).

and fields, streams and cliffs, rain and sunshine of the state of Baden as Sartre's philosophy is at home in the city of Paris. This fact makes the two men alien to each other, I believe, far more than differences of language, talents, and interests. Anyone who reads "The Field Path" with care cannot doubt that Heidegger's inspiration derives from his boyhood studies on that roughhewn bench under the oak tree, with its view of wide sloping fields ringed by the trees of the Black Forest in the distance. "As you began, so you will remain" according to Hölderlin in his "Hymn to the Rhine."[3] The path itself spoke to him, as he writes, encouraged him to decipher the thoughts in the books he found too hard to comprehend. The field path taught him to conceive of thinking itself as a path, and of man's brief career in time likewise as a path. The poet in him was quick to draw analogies among these physical paths through fields and forests and those of thinking and meditation in interior dialogue. They hindered the tendency to conceive of man as prime mover and shaper of his environment, which is a temptation for the city-bred youth. Instead, the predominance of rural life in and around his village helped the imaginative boy, and later philosophic thinker, to understand his intimations in the context of nature and her creations— man as the shepherd, not the master of things. Heidegger's consistent opposition to all forms of mere subjectivity in thinking is probably rooted in this enduring attachment to the processes of nature. The field path spoke to him, not he to the field path.

The boy was sent to the Gymnasium at Lake Constance sixty kilometers away, at that time the only youth to go from his village. Later he transferred to Freiburg and became involved at the university with Edmund Husserl

3. Quoted by Heidegger in his *Unterwegs zur Sprache* (Pfullingen: Gunther Neske, 1959), p. 93.

and gradually as an assistant and instructor in the complex tradition of German idealism. With the publication of *Sein und Zeit*, this inexperienced country boy suddenly became a famous professor. Both the professoriate and his philosophic tradition tended to complicate and "deform" the simple man. There is a professional deformation—I am not using the term in a moral sense—about academic life everywhere, though we who are in it are rarely aware of it sufficiently. It is perhaps particularly insidious and powerful in old Europe. The German philosophic tradition, despite its great merits, is too often devoted to abstractions and is obscure in expression. German professors lead lives that are sheltered and remote from the practical realities of daily existence. These deformations of institution and tradition worked their will on Heidegger. The early fame and later disgrace of his brief Nazi involvement contributed their part. His attempts to break out of these forms and deformations, to get into the open, as he likes to put it, seem to be attempts to recapture the early simplicities of his youth.

There is in Heidegger a lasting tension between the learned philosopher and the original thinker. This contrast is stated well in his poem: "Few of us are experienced enough in the difference between an object of scholarship and a matter of thought." Though his major writings are concerned with learned subjects, his deepest interest lies with that which is peculiar to his own thinking, going beyond the tradition, undeformed by it. His passion is for flashes of insight, which he seeks to distill in single words, phrases, and striking metaphors. As a thinker he wants to be simple in the manner of Socrates, whom he once called "the purest thinker of the West."[4]

4. Martin Heidegger, *Was heisst Denken?* in *What Is Called Thinking?*, trans. Fred D. Wieck and J. Glenn Gray (New York: Harper & Row, 1968), p. 17.

According to Heidegger, Socrates was purest because he constantly exposed himself to the full winds of reality and refused to run for cover by writing down his thoughts. Unlike Socrates in most respects, as we all know, Heidegger nevertheless cherishes the piety of that Socrates who dared to raise questions about things everyone else held as self-evident. More important still, he cherishes that Socrates who knew that human wisdom counts for little in the face of what we do not know, a knowledge Socrates bore with cheerfulness. Mystery is one of the basic words in the recent Heidegger. It is not for him a religious word, pointing toward some supersensible reality, but a philosophical one conveying the inexhaustibility of everyday things, which in our brief lives we can hardly make a start at fathoming.

## II

Heidegger identifies the simple with the original and consequently insists on the difference between the beginning, understood historically, and the origin, understood ontologically. An original insight into what really is, he asserts, often becomes obscured even by the time it commences its historical career. If we are to rediscover it and advance its implications, we must get behind this historical beginning, as it were. The simple in thinking is thus identified with that which is basic or fundamental in reality. To get at these fundamental structures and interrelationships requires a stripping away of the concealments of historical development. Heidegger believes that if we can reach the roots of a matter or, to employ his idiom, the sun and soil that nourish these roots, we shall discover that the true natures of things reveal themselves.

"The oldest of the old follows behind us in our thinking," as he puts it in his poem, "and yet it comes to meet us." Hence the oldest of the old can become the newest of the new. He likes to call this "recalling and responding thinking" *(das andenkende Denken)*, or lately, "strict" thinking. It possesses a double nature but is not ambiguous in a pejorative sense. Such thinking thinks back to the origin but in doing so responds to the call of Being as presence and present. The thinking back or remembering need not concern itself with what is first in time—with the pre-Socratics in philosophy, for example. It can equally well pertain to the hidden and perduring nature of a wine jug or a bridge, a contemporary poem by Trakl or a painting by Van Gogh. When strict thinking reaches behind the usual and traditional conceptions of such simple things, it can at times gain astonishing insights into what has not been thought before.

However, the simple is anything but easy or immediately available. As Heidegger says in the essay "Building Dwelling Thinking,"[5] its discovery requires "long experience and incessant practice." This discipline of experience and practice implies two things. First, a capacity to get involved in and to stay with a matter to be thought and, second, the ability to let it be what it truly is. The first of these capacities demands a singlemindedness and persistence that goes against the grain of all but the most select minds. Getting involved in something to be thought means living with it, making its pursuit a way of life rather than a problem to be solved. Thinking, as he puts it, is a way of dwelling, and dwelling is in turn a kind of building. To build well we must first acquire the grace to be at home in our region, to live into it, one could say. And both building and dwelling imply this strict thinking

5. Martin Heidegger, "Bauen Wohnen Denken" in the collected essays *Vorträge und Aufsätze* (Pfullingen: Gunther Neske, 1954).

that thinks back and responds to the call present to it. Pursuit of the simple in the craft of thinking, hence, needs long experience and large practice in living and building properly. Patience is necessary, a patience that outlasts the years.

Yet it would be false to understand this concentration and practice in thinking as an effort of will in a metaphysical sense. It is precisely the idea of the will as the ultimate source of reality which Heidegger constantly opposes and conceives to be a chief error of the German idealistic tradition. The *letting*, in "letting oneself into a matter" or "becoming involved with it," is of central importance. For it signifies a refusal to twist or distort that thought by personal presuppositions or a world view. The letting is a giving heed and an obedience to what is there in front of us. It is a capacity to hear and to see what is there and what there is. It is a letting go, a release of our self-will, which is at least as difficult to achieve as the becoming involved in, and staying with, the matter to be thought. What Heidegger is aiming at in this endeavor to think the simple in its origin, to think behind the beginning, is at once intensity and equanimity. There is a gathering of all our powers in mind and memory, a gathering which enables us to be open to what is truly in being and to perceive what is in being as it really is.

One might say that this openness and release are characteristic of great poets, whereas concentration and intensity characterize great thinkers. But poets require concentration, too, in the making of their poetry as thinkers require release. Only when these capacities are made into one, not merely added to each other, are we likely to get either true poets or true thinkers. At all events, what Heidegger is aiming at in his strict thinking, the thinking that recalls and responds, is precisely the indistinguishable unity of poet and thinker. Strict thinking is poetic thinking and for that reason not logical thinking; it is more encompassing and rigorous than the logical.

What are we to say to this attempt to get behind the beginning via a poetic thinking, at once intense and released, open to things as they are yet persistently single-minded? Perhaps many of us agree that the blend of concentration and release is a proper method of thinking either for poets or analytical scientists without agreeing at all that such thinking gets behind the beginning and hence is able to attain insights into the real. Certainly there is no assurance that insights will come and there is danger that such thinking will mistake the historical for the original, or even fall into nonsense.

And yet every original thinker thinks behind the beginning in some sense, for that is the meaning of the word origin and its adjective original. He starts without a compass, whereas scholars remain within the secure boundaries of learned subject matter. Original thinkers risk living on the boundaries, risk the abyss, as Nietzsche would say, on the frail chance of discovering the radically new. We should recognize that advances in understanding are frequently made by leaps of thought as well as by continuities. I do not know about Kierkegaard's leap of faith, having never made it, but I am persuaded that there are genuinely new possibilities in philosophy as in the sciences. The emphasis on "the leap," grown fashionable since Kierkegaard, is hardly more than our groping awareness that discontinuities are a persisting feature of modern life and thought. Who among us has not been impressed by the fragmentary knowledge of philosophy's past, possessed by a Kant or a Wittgenstein? And no one would assert that they discovered only what had long since been known.

To repeat: "Few of us are sufficiently experienced in the difference between a subject learned and a matter thought." The uncertainty that besets original thinking is, to quote the poem again, that "it must think against itself, which it can only seldom do." Why? Because learned subject matter gets in the way, the weight of past knowledge becomes burdensome, and the thought intrudes: who am I to set myself against the authority of that past which has made me who I am? Perhaps the sense of thinking against oneself can be well described as the assertiveness of the *I* over the *me* in the inner dialogue each of us carries on constantly. The established self in us resists, in this dialogue with the I, any radical confrontation with the unthought and the dangerously original. The dialogue, so far as the I is concerned, is genuine; the I has no interest in rejecting the me or tradition. But it is also not interested in agreement or surrender to the acquired and adapted self. It is willing to risk nonsense for the sake of new sense. For this reason, so I believe, there is much dross amidst the gold of all original thought. Lasting poetry and philosophy, too, hovers constantly on the brink between sense and nonsense. He who has not learned how to sort out the core of profound sense from the nonsense of an original thinker's works will be closed off from a great deal. The necessity for severe critical acumen is as great in studying an original thinker as it is in studying a scholar, for what gives itself out as original often turns out to be a mere reworking of the already known. This is surely as true for men like Rousseau, Kafka, and Kierkegaard as it is for Plato, Kant, and Heidegger, though I do not intend any comparative judgments by saying this.

What, we may ask, is so splendid about the simple? Clearly it does not lie in any surpassing of the already acquired. When an apprentice works his way to the status of journeyman and then with good fortune becomes his own master one fine day, the splendor of that achievement can hardly be sought in a triumph over the apprentice's teacher. We would not say that El Greco, in becoming his own man, surpassed his master, Titian. Nor did Aristotle surpass Plato any more than Heidegger surpassed Husserl. Nor does the splendor lie in any achievement of individuality over communality and tradition. There is something irrelevant, I believe, about individuality in original creation, however important individuality is in other spheres.

The discovery of the simple is a laying bare of the essential connections of things of the world and of our belonging to them. And its splendor lies in the new light this laying bare brings to us who experience it afresh. That person who enables us to get a fresh glimpse into the simple togetherness of things makes us participants in his discovery, not mere observers. And such insights simplify our own lives, making irrelevant much that had previously complicated them. Insofar as insight into essential relations can be called a feeling or an enduring mood, it brings about a kind of lightness and freedom from the weight and construction of the complicated. In this regard Heidegger recently called my attention to the fact that his basic word *Lichtung,* which we have been translating as "clearing" and "lighting," stemming from *aletheia,* the uncovering of truth, also signifies a lightening as when a boat weighs anchor and gains the freedom of the open water.

Something similar to this happens to our dispositions when we attain vision of some of man's innumerable relations to his context or surroundings. The experience of the splendor of simple things is more than a feeling, to be sure, and it is certainly not less. Perhaps this explains the otherwise unaccountable lifting of spirits we know in seeing a great tragedy on the stage whose denouement portrays destruction of the protagonists. Truth, however sad, has this capacity to enlighten in the twofold sense of illuminating our careers in time and making them easier to bear. *Veritas liberat,* as our college mottoes have it, but we do not always remember that *veritas* makes our burdens lighter by the glimpses it affords into fundamental relations that unite us to things and fellow men.

## III

In pursuit of such simplicity and its attendant splendor the later Heidegger is more and more inclined to follow that strand of our tradition extending from Heraclitus through Socrates to Nietzsche which insists that the discovery of truth involves a discarding of everything academic and scholarly that would cover up these essential relations. These academic traditions are even worse—because pretentious—than the tyrannical sway of "common sense" and the average man's preoccupation with narrowly utilitarian considerations. For the scholar in philosophy, according to Heidegger, has not only forgotten that the truth of the simplest things is hidden from us, but he has also forgotten that he has forgotten. This double forgetfulness makes it impossible for scholars to acknowledge truth as a mystery with which we must contend. Such forgetfulness likewise makes for pride in man's ability to bring forth these hidden relations on his own orders, as it were. Heidegger's harsh criticisms of our technological civilization are polemics against such pretensions. He identifies the hidden source of these pretensions as the belief that everything, including man, is producible on order, a belief he traces back to the metaphysical tradition of a transpersonal will as the source of all reality. Modern technologists, according to him, are the contemporary exemplars of a *hubris* that the Greeks chastised as the fount of human evil.

Against the pretensions of his German heritage, whose archexemplar is Hegel, for Heidegger the task of philosophy lies in this simple kind of meditative thinking, at once poetic and rigorous. Hegel wanted to change philosophy's nature by making it science—that is, knowledge certain of itself and completely self-aware. Philosophy, wrote Hegel, must put aside its name of being love of wisdom and become wisdom itself in the form of absolute knowledge. Heidegger seeks to reverse this overweening claim and to transform philosophy into something much more preliminary and "poverty-stricken" than even the love of wisdom. At the close of the *Letter on Humanism* he writes that "it is time for us to stop overestimating philosophy and therefore overtaxing it. In our present time of need we require less philosophy but more attentiveness to thinking, less literature but more cultivation of the letters themselves."[6]

This tentative and preliminary kind of thinking, which has increasingly captured Heidegger's mind over the past decades,

(1) cannot bring knowledge as do the sciences, (2) does not produce usable practical wisdom, (3) solves no cosmic riddles, (4) does not endow us directly with the power to act. As long as we still subject thinking to these four demands we shall overrate and overtax it. Both excesses prevent us from returning to a no longer customary modesty and to persist in it, amid the bustle of a civilization that daily clamors for a fresh supply of the latest novelties, and daily chases after excitement.[7]

6. Martin Heidegger, "Brief über den Humanismus" in *Wegmarken* (Frankfurt am Main: Vittorio Klostermann, 1967). First published in *Platons Lehre von der Wahrheit. Mit einem Brief über den Humanismus* (Bern: A. Francke, 1947).

7. *What Is Called Thinking?*, p. 159.

Here and elsewhere in his writings there is a clear renunciation of the confident claims for philosophy, not
merely of Heidegger's German tradition but also of the
claims of Plato and Aristotle, indeed most of the occi-
dental heritage. This renunciation is not, however, for
him a loss in any sense. "Renunciation does not take anything from us, but gives to us—the inexhaustible power
of the simple."[8]

Such renunciation of philosophy's claims is in no sense
a Stoic resignation nor is it an ancient or modern skep-
ticism concerning the powers of the mind to reach truth
and reality. Similarly his "step back" out of metaphysics
is not a denial of the work that German metaphysics carried on but rather an attempted new start at thinking
more originally about the soil and sun from which the
metaphysical tree has sprung. Heidegger's endeavor to
get to the inexhaustible power of the simple is as always
an attempt to think behind the beginning and to lay bare
the simple relations that inhere in Being and being human. To think behind the beginning is a striving to reach
that nonconceptual and nonrepresentational thinking of
the founders of Western thought, Pindar and Homer as
well as Heraclitus and Parmenides. In his preoccupation
with the notion of *Ereignis,* a crucial experience of the
later Heidegger, he thinks of an event that envisions man
and appropriates him to itself, rather than the other way
round. It is as though Being as a happening looks at us
and gathers us to itself. This is the sense of his much
misunderstood "turning," *die Kehre.*[9]

How does he propose by this renunciation to reach
"the inexhaustible power of the simple"? In a word the
answer runs: to learn how to live with or to stay close

8. *Der Feldweg,* p. 7.
9. I owe this insight into the significance of thinking behind
the beginning to a recent conversation with Hannah Arendt.

to things. The pieces in *Vorträge und Aufsätze,* titled
"Thing," "Building Dwelling Thinking," and ". . . Poetically Man Dwells . . ." provide a further elucidation of
this answer. To learn how to get close to and stay with
a thing requires learning, first of all. It does not come
easily or of itself. The real nature of a jug or bridge has
a way of eluding us, revealing itself only to those pre-
pared to attend and be obedient to its message; to them
it comes only in lightning flashes. Heidegger takes Heraclitus' gnomic saying "nature loves to hide" very seriously. Things cannot be brought near and their secrets
learned by people who treat them as utilitarian objects to
be used and used up, without ever giving them a search-
ing look or a thought that lingers on that look.

To be close to things immediately about us, whether
they be things of nature or made by man, requires us to
live poetically on earth—earth understood in the concrete sense of soil, trees, and seasons. This capacity is
more than the rapt attention of the child and the dreamy
fantasy of young lovers, much more. It demands also the
meditative capacity of a larger experience to discover a
new innocence of eye and mind that will let things be as
they are in themselves and hence enable us to be with
them, rather than they with us.

To live with things, furthermore, is hardly possible for
the rationalizing, grasping intellect of the philosopher
with his predilection for universalizing and his fatal love
of theory in the modern sense, so different from the
Greek seeing and sensing *(theoria).* Things are likewise
closed off to the analytic proclivities of natural scientists
who reduce everything to chlorophyl, to atoms, or generally to objects which scientists as subjects seek to cap-
ture in their isolated particularity. In Heidegger's pursuit
of the simple and its power there is nearly as great an

aversion to scientific dissection as to philosophical "theory."

Things are lived with properly and come near to us, says Heidegger, when they are tended, preserved, cared for, "saved." This does not preclude use, to be sure, since only in proper use does the hidden nature of any thing come into its own. In his superb description of a Greek temple in the long essay "The Origin of the Work of Art,"[10] Heidegger succeeds in making vivid the way in which stone, wood, and metal, the surf, the wind, and clouds, the men and animals and the god within the temple are all brought into their true nature by the way this work of art discloses a world and uncovers the truth at work in the art work. In this profounder sense he understands the activities of saving and guarding. They are separated by a wide gulf from the exploitation of things as mere materials for our profit. There is all the difference between the person who uses up something thoughtlessly as an object and the artist who tends and attends to it with a view to bringing forth its latent potentialities.

So carried away by the possibility of flashing insight through compliant attention to things does Heidegger become that he conceives them as powers which gather into themselves the fourfold world of earth and sky, divinities and mortals. *Die Dinge dingen*, "Things 'thing,'" he writes, and has thus exposed himself to the ridicule of the popular German press. Had Leibniz enjoyed (or suffered) a popular press in his time, his doctrine of the monads, each of which mirrors the world in its fashion

10. Martin Heidegger, *Der Ursprung des Kunstwerkes. Mit einer Einführung von Hans-Georg Gadamer* (Stuttgart: Philipp Reclam Jun., 1960), pp. 41–43. First published in *Holzwege* (Frankfurt am Main: Vittorio Klostermann, 1950).

and is nevertheless without windows, would doubtless have evoked similar hilarity.

Things thing. That is, they gather to themselves the permanent and the transient of our world, the animate and inanimate, the near and the remote, the sacred and the secular. These phenomena are manifest in whatever particular thing we pay heed to by tending and sparing it. If one studies Heidegger, as opposed to reading him only, and if one seeks to link this thought of his, that a thing gathers together the world, to his philosophy as a whole, I believe it will lose much of its outlandish character and possibly count in the end as a genuine insight.

Despite his rejection of the German philosophic tradition, Heidegger is in this assertion about "thinging" its best representative in many respects. That tradition has ever been closely linked to the Greek; indeed the German poets and thinkers have often enough been accused of being enslaved to the Greeks. For both traditions certain ideas have been central. Two of these are the unity and intelligibility of the world as a whole. These two ideas are so closely interrelated, of course, that they are inseparable, even though they are far from being identical. The dominant themes of intelligibility and unity imply that both traditions seek to overcome commonsense disjunctions of subject and object or man and world. They accomplish it by conceiving man's mind as fitted to nature and the nonhuman by a kind of prerational harmony. By a more comprehensive view philosophic thinking tries to eliminate dualities of every kind in a process of nature, or *physis*, conceived as an active, ever-changing, yet perduring activity. Both traditions try to understand such primordial unity by thinking mind as an entelechy, a *telos* that pervades nature in every seam and pore and is only illustrated in man, not incorporated merely in our species. This is what is meant by intelligibility.

It is true that the Christian faith, with its radical disjunction between man and the rest of nature, played an important role in wrenching the German thinkers and poets away from Greek notions of intelligibility and unity. But with the onset of the Romantic movement the pagan Greek inspiration asserted itself anew. In Heidegger, as in many of his predecessors, including Hegel, one finds the conflict of the classic Greek emphasis on unity and intelligibility opposed to Christian transcendence and man-centeredness. Increasingly, however, the Greek vision of man as an integral part of nature wins out—in Heidegger more than in Hegel. Indeed the later Heidegger can best be understood as Hegel's antipode.

One thing more needs to be recalled in this thumbnail sketch. The Germans inherited from both the Greek and the Christian past a profound concern for individuality. They have by no means been willing to sacrifice on the altar of a seamless unity the particularity and uniqueness of individual otherness, though how to ground this unique particularity, confronted by the requirements of unity and intelligibility, has been a perennial problem for these thinkers.

Heidegger's assertion that things 'thing,' however bizarre it sounds, becomes clearer if we keep this long tradition in mind, and if we also remember his ceaseless attempts to get behind the beginning. Like the early Greeks—and unlike most of us since the rise of modern science—he thinks that mind and world are linked together in a fundamental way. This means that we have our being in things and are not confined within our skins. We stand through and into space; our beings are spatialized. As he puts it in the essay "Thing," those who attend to things are really closer to the famous old bridge in Heidelberg, however distant they may be in a geographical sense, than are many who cross over it every day without paying it any heed. He understands this in more than an imaginative sense (let me repeat), for ever since he worked out the brief section on the spatiality of *Dasein* in *Being and Time* he views man's relation to being as a standing *through* space, not simply *in* a given place.

Accordingly, by things thinging he wants to assert that they carry the power of uniting in an interplay the spatiality of earth, sky, divinities, and mortals—an interplay that at once preserves their individuality and their belonging together. By staying close to things, living with them in an attentive and thoughtful way, we too are drawn into this unity and can gain from it our individuality, our developing yet persisting nature. All this, Heidegger admits, is not graspable in a concept (concept means in German a grasping, as it also does in the Latin root of our word "concept"). But it is also not merely an imaginative act, if imagination be understood as fantasy. For him it is the very marrow of the truly real. To understand it requires practice and experience in strict thinking that recalls the oldest of the old and responds to the newest of the not-yet which is coming toward us. One could say that Heidegger takes thinking poetry or poetic thinking with ultimate seriousness. "Singing and thinking," as he writes in the poem, "are the tree trunks neighbor to poetry. They grow out of Being and reach into its truth."

# IV

What are we to say to this kind of vision? Is it possible to subject it to meaningful philosophic criticism? Once it is understood can one disentangle the true from the false, the public and usable from the private and idiosyncratic? Some of us who have devoted many hours to the study of Heidegger's publications have a responsibility, it seems to me, to attempt an answer to these questions, even if their evasion would be more comfortable. Those who, like myself, are grateful to Heidegger for what they have learned from him and yet have no desire to be disciples of his should endeavor to say precisely what they have learned and why they are nevertheless unwilling to follow his path of thought.

Earlier I suggested that the splendor of the simple lies in its power to uncover essential relations of man to the world as it really is. Heidegger's thinking is ultimately simple in that he has seen and shown some of these relations, enabling us to attain a less psychological and more phenomenological orientation to the world we inhabit. His thought demonstrates what it is possible for a powerful and original mind to accomplish when it resolutely stays for a lifetime on a single theme and within a regional context, devoting itself to boring deep beneath the surface of the received tradition and ways of life of southwest Germany. I have no doubt that many of Heidegger's insights brought to the surface as a result of this close attending and persisting are profound and enduring, capable of indefinite further development and enrichment in areas of knowledge usually remote from philosophy.

But there are strong negative aspects to this so-called rigorous thinking of Heidegger and to the whole program of simplicity in thought. It is indeed difficult for philosophic criticism to evaluate the poetic thinking of the later Heidegger. The implicit command here is: take it or leave it untouched—that is, think in this way or think conceptually and representationally. If you choose the second alternative, you will never be able to understand poetic thinking. There is a severe weakness in any method or path on the way to truth which makes such a presupposition as this. Let us make no mistake about it. No thinking, poetic or logical, ought to lay claim to immunity from criticism when that criticism is equally involved and impartial.

There is something quite seductive about the appeal to simplicity in the poetic, declamatory statement. We experience this seductivity in the ringing words of Jesus and "the one thing needful" of his ethical teachings, his sermon on the mount. The Western world has for centuries been captivated by the grand simplicity of Jesus' program for the good life and yet utterly unable to live according to these teachings. Perhaps only in our time are we coming to realize the insufficiency of Christian ethics in itself in contrast to our own inadequacies. In all of us there is an inextinguishable inclination to glorify the simple in the face of the baffling complexities of actual existence.

Simple things are not alone in revealing splendor. Earlier I suggested that Hegel's philosophy is the antipode to Heidegger, especially the later Heidegger. No one would suggest that Hegel is simple. Yet I believe that his systematic and comprehensive vision possesses its own splendor. As we struggle to comprehend the turbulent social scene of today there is surely much to be learned from Hegel. His current revival in the West is an unwitting testimony to this fact. Hegel studied the wide range of political and historical realities of his time and then sought to combine them into a whole whose truth resides not in those parts but in their interrelationships. If he yielded to the excessive pride of believing that philosophy could slough off the title love of wisdom and become wisdom itself, our reaction to this need not be the Heideggerian rejection of practical wisdom and return to a thinking that makes no claim to "endow us directly with the power to act." I at least am emphatically unwilling to surrender philosophy's ancient claim to being a guide to conduct and the examined life. Such renunciation on the part of Heidegger appears to take something from us in fact, despite his assertion that it gives us "the inexhaustible power of the simple." I have never been satisfied that his justly celebrated *Letter on Humanism* came to grips with Jean Beaufret's question concerning a possible ethics arising from Heidegger's ontology. Splendid as that *Letter* surely is, it does not go far enough to reach the truly concrete in Hegel's sense.

There is, after all, a limit to what we can accomplish with a few basic words and the single theme, that of Being in Heidegger's case. Hegel would hardly have said, as Heidegger does, that every thinker thinks one single thought. And the history of ideas would surely support Hegel on this point. Heidegger's method of circling around a single theme and boring deeper and deeper within it has unquestioned merit. But what one gains in depth, one loses in scope.

Though Hegel's thinking was history-oriented to an almost unparalleled degree, he never tired of reminding his fellow Germans that it was their task to understand the present, not the past. "Here is Rhodes, dance here" was his slogan. It was not that he loved the time in which he lived so much, for like Heidegger and so many of his own contemporaries his heart was fonder of the classic Greeks. But a hardheaded realism ruled that heart and bade him keep philosophy to the thankless task of interpreting present realities. One might remark, parenthetically, that such realism shielded him also against the utopianism of his left-wing successors.

I fear that Heidegger's thinking, despite himself, is too past-oriented. This may be the chief danger always in the pursuit of the simple and perhaps its great attractiveness.

Heidegger's regionalism is at once his strength and his weakness. He illustrates what a powerful and imaginative mind can draw of philosophic sustenance from attachment to home and the familiar things of use and beauty. But today we are living in a cosmopolitan world and are becoming nomads once more, exposing ourselves willy-nilly to the uncanny and unhomelike. It will not do for philosophy to lament this new situation, unwelcome as many of its features certainly are. Rather, a philosophy which cherishes practical wisdom must begin with these hard realities and by living close to them strive to make them more comprehensible to a baffled younger generation, drifting rapidly into an unfruitful self-alienation. Such nomadic thinking will not have the appeal that inheres in regional thought, but it will gain in realism and hardness and possibly interpret better man's true situation in all its comic and tragic dimensions.

It would be, however, a fatal mistake to assume that a new way of thinking (which I have called nomadic and will develop elsewhere) can dispense with the legacy of home and specifically the legacy of a Heidegger. He himself is constantly enjoining us to think for ourselves, not to walk along his own paths or write dissertations about his works. In *What Is Called Thinking?* he cites Nietzsche's letter to George Brandes: "After you had discovered me, it was no trick to find me: the difficulty now is to lose me." And Heidegger remarks that after we have succeeded in finding Nietzsche's thought, we may well try to lose it again. "And this, to lose, is harder than to find; because 'to lose' in such a case does not just mean to drop something, leave it behind, abandon it. 'To lose' here means to make ourselves truly free of that which Nietzsche's thinking has thought."[11]

11. *What Is Called Thinking?*, p. 52.

Such a procedure holds equally well for Heidegger. We have, of course, hardly yet discovered him, much less understood him. But once this is accomplished, we should have the courage and independence of thought to clear our own paths. Only on such a course will full recognition be paid to the long and often lonely labors of an original thinker named Martin Heidegger.

# Poets and Thinkers: Their Kindred Roles in the Philosophy of Martin Heidegger

Someday the major significance of the existentialist movement may be seen to lie in the recovery of poetry (in the generic sense of imaginative literature and art) as a subject matter for philosophy. For many generations philosophers have looked to natural science for a model of philosophic method as well as for standards by which to judge the worth of philosophic effort. Anglo-Saxon philosophers have also used the findings of the sciences, social and natural, increasingly as the proper material for reflection—indeed as the very core of their discipline. In conceiving philosophy to be a criticism of culture, they

Reprinted from *Phenomenology and Existentialism* (Baltimore, Md.: The Johns Hopkins Press, 1967).

have been impelled to pay more and more attention to science as the enterprise that has revolutionized the modern world.

Literature has inevitably suffered by philosophers' devotion to the sciences. In America at least, and hardly less in Britain, it has become a mark of derogation to refer to a philosopher as essentially a poet. "I am an ignorant man, almost a poet," Santayana once remarked, and the remark is frequently understood in a sense which that ironic spirit did not intend. For the impression is inescapable that many, if not most, English-speaking philosophers not only consider poets ignorant of knowledge worth having—that is, scientific knowledge—but also find their utterances subjective and arbitrary. Poets do not tell us anything about the way things are in the world; they only reveal private moods. At most they celebrate values, whereas scientists and philosophers are charged with preserving and extending knowledge of nature and man.

This climate of opinion may be changing. With dismay many scientifically oriented philosophers have witnessed the rise to prominence of existentialism on the European continent since World War II. Even the British have turned away from preoccupation with science to the study of language, though not to the language of poetry. In an era when the effects of the scientific revolution are at their peak and in dire need of interpretation and mediation to the lay mind, is it not irresponsible of so many European philosophers to be looking to literature and language for the primary source of their eccentric analyses and doctrines? So it seems to many American academicians of philosophy. Yet history reveals, if we care to reflect, parallel instances of dramatic shifts of allegiance at unexpected times and places in the career of Western philosophy.

In the German tradition such a shift of allegiance hardly amounts to a revolution. Poets and philosophers have always been closely associated in Germany. It was Kant who insisted in his third *Critique* that for an adequate account of the world philosophers should investigate the ideas and visions of art and artists. As John Herman Randall has emphasized recently, it was Kant's *Critique of Judgment* that became a major source of inspiration for idealism and romanticism, which dominated the nineteenth century in Germany.[1] This close alliance of poetry and thought reached a peak but did not end in Schelling's conception of "productive imagination" as the way to philosophic wisdom. Later Germans such as Schopenhauer, Nietzsche, and most of the *Lebensphilosophen* preserved this alliance down to the present. "Poets and thinkers" is anything but a chance conjunction of terms in German intellectual history. When studying Nietzsche, Herder, Lessing, or many another German writer, it is difficult to discover where philosophy ends and poetry begins.

From this perspective Martin Heidegger's increasing preoccupation with the role of poetry in his philosophy is easily understandable. Though he is not a typical existentialist (if indeed he is one at all), his work has already been influential for the whole movement and likewise has had profound impact on the interpretation of literature and the other arts in Europe. In this respect, at least, Heidegger is far from revolutionary. On the contrary, he is a continuator of that long line of artist-philosophers which began in ancient Greece and which has long been so congenial to the German philosophic temperament. If we ever succeed in assimilating Heidegger's peculiar language, he may even become in the eyes of posterity a

1. John H. Randall, Jr., *The Career of Philosophy* (New York: 1965), II, Book V, 175, 176 *et passim*.

representative philosopher of the German tradition, if not of our whole era.

In what follows I want to sketch Heidegger's views, as they have developed over the years, on the interconnections of poetry and philosophy and the close affinities of poets and philosophers for each other. I shall try to clarify why he considers the utterances of poets like Hölderin, Trakl, and Sophocles of such importance for philosophy. If I am successful, the attempt should throw some light on the general shift of allegiance from science to art, particularly the art of literature, which I believe to be characteristic of existentialist thought.

It is best to begin with Heidegger's conception of the essential task of philosophy, though "mission" perhaps would be the more appropriate word. This task he has stated very explicitly in a lecture series at Freiburg in the middle thirties, published in 1953 under the title *Einführung in die Metaphysik*.[2]

In the opening lecture Heidegger defines his conception of philosophy by first rejecting two current misconceptions of its function. The first of these is the demand that philosophy provide a foundation upon which a nation can build its historical life and culture. This asks too much of a philosophy, Heidegger insists, for "philosophy can never *directly* supply the energies and create the opportunities and methods that bring about a historical change."[3] The second misconception somewhat more modestly conceives philosophy as a cultural force because it provides an over-all view of the premises, basic concepts, and principles of the sciences. "Philosophy thus is

2. *An Introduction to Metaphysics*, trans. Ralph Manheim (New Haven: 1959; New York: 1961). In the quotations used I have generally followed Manheim's translation, taken from the Doubleday Anchor edition, except for his rendering of *das Seiende* and *das Sein*.

3. Manheim, p. 8.

expected to promote and even accelerate—to make easier, as it were—the practical and technical business of culture."[4] According to Heidegger this second misinterpretation distorts the real function of philosophy.

In opposition to these views Heidegger believes that "philosophy is one of the few autonomous creative possibilities and at times necessities of man's historical existence."[5] It is not dependent on other disciplines nor is its mission to provide a systematic cultural perspective. No, philosophy must break new paths, open new perspectives, bring into radical question the very foundation of the values and norms by which a people live. By thinking more deeply and simply, philosophy must challenge conventional ways of viewing the world and thereby provide a more authentic knowledge of things than any social or natural science can achieve. The advance of any civilization tends to cover up and obscure man's fundamental relations to his environment and to his fellows. Hence philosophy's mission is to break new paths into strange and unfamiliar terrain—terrain that has become unfamiliar because a people forgets continually the points of reference of its historical existence and needs to be recalled to them.

In this connection Heidegger quotes Nietzsche, to whom he is clearly indebted for this conception of philosophy, with approval. "A philosopher is a man who never ceases to experience, see, hear, suspect, hope, and dream extraordinary things. . . ." "Philosophy . . . is a voluntary living amid ice and mountain heights."[6] The concern with philosophy, Heidegger continues, is of necessity restricted to the few, because only those of great spirit have eyes for the extraordinary and sufficient courage to bring the

4. Manheim, p. 9.
5. Manheim, p. 8.
6. Manheim, pp. 10, 11.

foundations into question. Though in later decades he has come to reject, I believe, Nietzsche's emphasis on the extraordinary nature of philosophy's subject matter in favor of meditating on the simple and commonplace objects of experience, he has certainly retained this basic conception of the essence of philosophic thinking as creative and pathbreaking.

It was in these lectures on metaphysics—rather than in his earlier *Sein und Zeit*—that Heidegger began to concern himself with the pre-Socratics, Parmenides and Heraclitus in particular, and to combine them with a long discussion of Sophocles' famous chorus from the *Antigone.* Here poets and thinkers were pathbreakers par excellence; they taught us what it means really to think, not simply in terms of ethics, metaphysics, or any of the later divisions of philosophy which first came into existence in fifth-century Athens. Heidegger is convinced that crucial and originative thinking tends to cease when thinkers turn into philosophers—that is, into those who are professionally taught to think. Scholarship in philosophy is a necessary and useful occupation, he tells us in *Was heisst Denken?* but there is no guarantee that the philosophically learned know what thinking is. The pre-Socratics, on the other hand, were not learned men, but they knew how to think, Heidegger believes, as do few of us today. Indeed, the sentence that becomes a recurring refrain in *Was heisst Denken?* is: "The most thought-provoking thing in our thought-provoking age is that we are still not thinking."[7]

Why does he believe that these earliest philosophers of the West, who lived before the very name "philosophy" was coined, are the models of what thinking ought to be? To provide a full answer to this question would exceed by

7. *Was heisst Denken?* (Tübingen: 1954), p. 3 *et passim.*

far the limits of this essay. But to get at the essential relations of poetry and thinking, as he conceives them, it is necessary to suggest the outlines of an answer.

These first thinkers were concerned with *physis*, that fundamental reality which the Romans translated as *Natura*—thus perverting, so Heidegger thinks, the basic subject matter of philosophy, a perversion that endured throughout the Middle Ages and into modern times. Men like Anaximander, Parmenides, and Heraclitus conceived *physis* as "self-blossoming emergence . . . that which manifests itself in such unfolding and perseveres and endures in it. . . . *Physis*, the realm of that which arises, is not synonymous with these phenomena, which today we regard as part of 'nature' . . . *Physis* is Being itself, by virtue of which existing things become and remain observable."[8]

Unencumbered with learning and pseudo-sophistication, the pre-Socratics were clear-sighted enough to perceive the whole of that which is and the parts within that whole in their essential relations to it. They did not confuse Being with single existents, or believe that Being is nothing more and nothing other than the sum total of single existents, the later view of metaphysicians whom Heidegger opposes. Moreover, their basic problem was to think this vision of totality adequately, to discover the integral relation of *physis* and *logos,* indeed to uncover the belonging-together of Being and language. "It is in words and language," Heidegger asserts, "that things first come into being and are. For this reason the misuse of language in idle talk, in slogans and phrases, destroys our authentic relation to things."[9] Their thinking was prior to the scholarly separation of subject and object, hence prior to any separation of poetic and scientific

8. Manheim, pp. 11, 12.
9. Manheim, p. 11.

thought. The pre-Socratics thought about the things of nature and man from the standpoint of the mighty spectacle itself, not the other way around. As he puts it in the *Introduction to Metaphysics*:

> The Greeks did not learn what *physis* is through natural phenomena, but the other way around: it was through a fundamental poetic and intellectual experience of Being that they discovered what they had to call *physis*. It was this discovery that enabled them to gain a glimpse into nature in the restricted sense. Hence *physis* originally encompassed heaven as well as earth, the stone as well as the plant, the animal as well as man, and it encompassed human history as a work of men and the gods; and ultimately and first of all, it meant the gods themselves as subordinated to destiny. *Physis* means the power that emerges and the enduring realm under its sway. This power of emerging and enduring includes "becoming" as well as "being" in the restricted sense of inert duration. *Physis* is the process of arising, of emerging from the hidden, whereby the hidden is first made to stand.[10]

The above paragraph puts more clearly than any other I have been able to find the significance of the pre-Socratics for Heidegger. It also hints at the notion of what genuine thinking is, which he develops in later works. He does not want us to return to the pre-Socratics for the sake of their discoveries but to recover their stance as thinkers. This stance was one of simplicity, astonishment, and openness to the world as world. Only by returning to this stance will we be in a position to make a leap into the kind of thinking that will reveal our world to us as theirs was revealed to them. A thinker's task is to reveal Being, according to him, and relate it to, and distinguish it from, single existents and their sum.

This task can be accomplished only by means of a

10. Manheim, p. 12.

poetic and intellectual experience, similar to that given to the pre-Socratics. In such later works as *Was heisst Denken?*, *Holzwege,* and *Vorträge und Aufsätze* Heidegger has come to grasp this kind of experience in terms of man's learning to dwell rightly on earth. Dwelling and a capacity for dwelling rightly have come to have for him the ontological sense and weight that being-in-the-world held for him in the earlier *Sein und Zeit* period.[11] If the fundamental characteristic of dwelling is care-taking, as he emphasizes in a key essay of the last-named volume, the activities that constitute care-taking are thinking and building. Let me first characterize briefly what he conceives to be the essence of thinking before I turn to his discussion of poets and poetry.

Thinking is called or bidden into existence by what there is to think about, and this, in the broadest sense, is Being itself. Being, however, is not something that lies behind appearances, but *is* their face or countenance. The truth of things shines in their appearance; it is the elusive substance of appearance. We must look for the truth of Being in the intricate structures and manifold phenomena of this motley world, of which man is so inextricably a part. In the phenomena of our cultural past the thinker must discover the unthought elements in every previous system if he is not to miss the essential and authentic. In the phenomena of nature he must seek to penetrate the disguises of appearance and come upon the necessary relations and abiding powers. Truth is an uncovering or revelation of what is, but there is always still another veil or cover concealing the essential. As Hei-

11. Compare Vincent Vycinas, *Earth and Gods: An Introduction to the Philosophy of Martin Heidegger* (The Hague: 1961). I am indebted to Vycinas for this point and at several other places in this essay. His scholarly study of the later Heidegger deserves to be known better than it is at present.

degger expresses it, Being is always advancing toward
man (who is, when authentic, open to its message), but
it is retreating, too. Its uncovering is at one and the same
time a covering up and obscuring of its essence. Words
conceal as well as reveal it, whether the phenomenon in
question is a philosophic system of the past, a technological civilization of today, or nature itself as yet untouched by human building or poetizing.

Hence the thinker must be at once receptive and
assertive, fully focused on what is there to be perceived.
He must know how to listen and to observe, for thinking
in the first instance is not so much an activity that we
initiate as it is something that is initiated by *physis*, or
Being itself. He must learn how to be astonished by what
he perceives, as the early Greeks were astonished. This
implies an attitude of openness far more fundamental
than the usual meaning of the word. It is not "a listening
with the inner ear" or other such metaphorical ways of
expression. Rather it is a belonging of the whole being
to what is to be thought about and at the same time a
collecting, or re-collecting, in language of the abiding
powers that inform our mortal natures. Man is in essence
a pointer, as he reminds us in *Was heisst Denken?*, a
signpost which reveals this ever advancing and retreating
phenomenon of the world whole.

Authentic thinking is far more simple than we complicated modern men imagine. We have not learned to
think as yet because we do not know how to face the
world as world, to understand the essence of a simple
thing like a jug or a bridge, which assembles, focuses,
this world for us. The difficulty, he seems to say, lies in
us, in our inability to listen to what words in their primordial nature tell us about these objects. That is, we do not
focus ourselves and our words rightly. For we possess in
the immense power of language and in our primary

inclination toward truth the necessary equipment by which to approach Being. We do not know how to think or to build because of our lack of attunement and rootedness. To dwell close to things and approach them in their own nature involves a determination to let them be what they are—namely, the assemblage of the durable powers of the earth.

Heidegger is convinced that poets can come to the aid of thinkers now, when the latter are so out of touch with the sources of Being. The importance of poetry has steadily grown in his estimation to the point where it appears to overshadow systematic philosophic analysis. In *Sein und Zeit* we read comparatively little of poets and art works. But with his Hölderlin essays of the thirties, references to poets and poetic utterances have increased so markedly that one wonders whether Heidegger has not discovered in poetry the way to overcome that "inadequacy" in the language of traditional philosophy which prevented him, as he claimed, from completing the second half of *Sein und Zeit*.

It should be emphasized, however, that turning to poetry does not signify that Heidegger is concerned with aesthetics per se. His interest in poets is for their ontological significance, the truths they can teach us about man's way of dwelling on earth. Strictly speaking, he does not treat imaginative literature and other works of art *qua* literature and art but as aspects of philosophy or meditative thought. In the last essay of the collection of lectures *Unterwegs zur Sprache* (1959), he puts this most succinctly: "All reflective thought is poetic: all poetry, however, is thought."[12] This progressive unity of function of poets and thinkers is an important development of his philosophy. At one time, following Hölderlin,

12. *Unterwegs zur Sprache* (Pfullingen: 1959), p. 267.

he believed that "poets and thinkers dwell near to one another, on peaks farthest apart." The function of poets was to name the holy—that is, the essential powers of nature—and the function of thinkers was to think Being. It would be fair to say that recently these peaks on which poets and thinkers dwell have come very close to each other.

Nevertheless, this sameness of function in poets and thinkers, Heidegger warns, must never be taken in the sense of identity, of an empty and mathematical oneness. The concept "identical," or "undifferentiated," is always quite different from the concept of "same." Things can be the same in the sense that they are inseparable from each other yet far from identical; there is a belonging-together of different qualities in an organic and primary unit. One can speak of the same, he writes, only when one thinks of the differences. So it is with poetry and thought. Poets and thinkers think the same but not the identical. Both are intent on discerning the powers of the earth and the sky, of mortals and gods, of *physis* and *logos*. Their differences lie in the way they conceive these powers and in the formulation of their thoughts.[13]

What specific role does poetry have for Heidegger in the task or mission of philosophy? Perhaps his most systematic statement of this role is to be found in the first long essay of *Holzwege,* entitled "Der Ursprung des Kunstwerkes."[14] In this essay he concentrates on the function of the work of art in assembling the world for us.

The lines of Hölderlin that Heidegger most frequently quotes in his attempts to express man's relation to being are these:

13. *Vorträge und Aufsätze* (Pfullingen: 1954), p. 193.
14. Translated by Albert Hofstadter as "The Origin of the Artwork" in *Philosophies of Art and Beauty,* ed. Albert Hofstadter and Richard Kuhns (New York: 1964).

Voll Verdienst, doch dichterisch, wohnet
Der Mensch auf dieser Erde.

These have been variously translated by Michael Hamburger[15] as

Full of profit but poetically man
Lives on this earth.

and by Douglas Scott[16] as

Full of merit, and yet poetically, dwells
Man on this earth.

As is his wont, Heidegger gives ontological weight to each of the words in these lines. He has even devoted an entire essay in *Vorträge und Aufsätze* to the portion of them that reads "poetically, dwells/Man on this earth." Perhaps the best way to reach the substance of his conception of the role of poetry in philosophy is to summarize his analysis of this line.

Poets teach us how to dwell on the earth because their language is concrete and exact. They are our teachers, as Homer was to the early Greeks, in the sense of keeping us near the earth and attentive to the real powers that dominate our lives. Far from being the irresponsible and arbitrary creatures that the Philistine imagines, they are, according to Heidegger, the model men of any epoch because they seek to catch in words the essence of appearance. They name the enduring powers in nature and culture and learn to sing and celebrate that which really is. Not only are they more "present" than the majority of men, they are also more sensitive to the potentialities of

15. Michael Hamburger, *Hölderlin* (New York: 1952).
16. "Hölderin and the Essence of Poetry," trans. Douglas Scott, *Existence and Being,* by Martin Heidegger (Chicago: 1949).

language for revealing man to himself and for emphasizing his belonging to natural and social reality.

Moreover, poetry is "in a strict sense a measure or a standard by which man receives the measure for the width of his being."[17] Poets alone can teach us our limits—that is, what we can and cannot do. By establishing in words man's capacities in relation to the immense forces of nature around him, they teach him his mortality and make him capable of death as death. When really poetic and genuine, their words are not simply arbitrary; they are neither subjective nor objective but a true standard of man's situation in time and in the midst of nonhuman realities. Such utterance is the voice of being itself. Poets are more open than the rest of us and under no illusion that they are masters of language. Rather they allow language to speak through them. Heidegger quotes Hölderlin to the effect that "language, that most dangerous of possessions, has been given to man . . . so that he may affirm what he is."

In short, poets establish for us our human nature; they define us in relation to the earth and sky: They teach us to dwell rightly on earth, to make a home instead of merely inhabiting a series of houses; they teach us how to build properly, which is an activity of dwelling; and how to think instead of merely logicizing. And poets enable man to dwell by showing him how to be grateful and joyous for this possibility of dwelling. "Little knowledge, but much joy/Is given to mortals," sang Hölderlin, and Heidegger discovers that when one pursues thinking into its essential origin, thinking and thanking are much the same. If we can learn to dwell in the spirit of guarding and cherishing the earth, instead of exploiting and mastering it, we will learn that kind of gratitude which

17. *Vorträge und Aufsätze*, p. 196.

comes from "care," which Heidegger from the beginning of his career has conceived to be the most comprehensive essence of human nature. "The writing of poetry permits the act of dwelling initially to enter into its own nature. Poetry is the original letting-dwell."[18]

If one could put in a few words what Heidegger is saying about poets it would run something like this: Men are initially given to dwelling poetically on earth—that is, to perceiving things as they truly are—but every age requires poets, who are the most innocent of beings, to see more deeply into the nature of things and to bring them close to the sources of their being. Far from being subjective or arbitrary in their utterances, they are able to sing of phenomena as phenomena. They teach us to see more exactly, to glimpse *physis* in its unity with *logos* in a way that scholars, scientists, and practical men are unable to glimpse it. They are not knowers but seers, and Heidegger is persuaded that such seers are the sanest men of any epoch.

Do all men dwell poetically? No, he answers, but all men are capable of it to some degree. And they can actualize these potentials by listening to and learning from poets, whether they write in verse or prose. In fact, it is best if they speak rather than write. Nor is Heidegger talking of all "poets," but only of the authentic few who are thinking and poetizing in the proximity of Being itself.

It is evident that Heidegger's high estimation of the utterances of such selected poets is governed by two philosophical considerations: his conception of language and his theory of truth. To language Heidegger attributes a power that has rarely been accorded it by philosophers since the early Greeks. It was Aristotle who wrote that a thing is what it may be said to be. In the "Letter on

18. *Vorträge und Aufsätze*, p. 202.

Humanism" Heidegger calls language "the house of Being," which is, I take it, a contemporary expression of the Aristotelian position. *Logos* is not simply the way human beings reveal to themselves the appearances of *physis* or the world process but in an ontological sense is the same (not to say identical) with it.

Man is under an illusion, Heidegger keeps repeating, so long as he imagines he is the master of language. Instead, language masters him. When a person is genuinely concerned with speaking rather than merely chattering, he does not really determine what he says, but his speech is determined for him by Being, by the innermost essence of things. This faith in the powers of language to put us in touch with reality, not at the periphery but at its very center, has not been unexampled in the history of philosophic thought, but is, to say the least, uncommon in the modern world. In a climate of opinion where language is thought of as a tool or instrument of thought, Heidegger's conception testifies to the boldness and radicality of his philosophy. It is also testimony to the influence of the Greeks on him in an aspect of their thinking that has grown strange to us.

Sometimes it is said that Heidegger's philosophy can be understood only through his conception of truth as *aletheia*—uncovering or disclosure. This may well be so; in any event he has held without much change to this notion from his first works to his latest. Certainly this idea helps to explain the ever-closer relation between poetry and thinking which has undergone evolution in his philosophizing. Poetry, as we have seen, is of primary concern to him insofar as it reveals truth—that is, ontological truth or the truth of Being. Such truth is not approached through a long process either of deduction or induction. It is not the result of the work of science and scientists. Heidegger does not, of course, deny the reality or importance of the correspondence theory of truth. Nor does he reject the work of scholarship and science in their principal concern with the notion of truth as adequacy between intellect and thing. In its own sphere this notion of truth is inevitable, necessary, and very fruitful. But in the quest of ontological truth, he insists that the conception of *aletheia*, revelation in its secular meaning, is all-important.

Man knows primary Being not through the processes of logic or of scientific investigation. It is not a result either in the pragmatic sense or in that of sheer intellection. Empiricism and rationalism in their traditional roles are both inadequate. Truth is rather a kind of "seeing" reached by means of a leap out of man's habitual tendency to place himself as subject over against the world of objects. It is a leap into the midst of this world of things and a reading of the signs of the real displayed there, instead of an inventing of them as an outsider. Understood in this way, truth is more likely to reveal itself to innocent yet profound poetic natures than it is to highly sophisticated, self-conscious scholars or scientists. Hence for thinkers intent on ontological truth, poetry can be investigated more profitably than highly learned works. And nature herself can reveal the same truth when approached by thinkers without preconceptions. In his essay "Remembrance of the Poet," Heidegger writes of Lake Constance in a way that reveals how closely he equates poetry and truth.

. . . Thus we still think of this water unpoetically. And how much longer are we going to? How long are we going to imagine that there was first of all a part of nature existing for itself and a landscape existing for itself, and that then with the help of "poetic experiences" this landscape became

colored with myth? How long are we going to prevent ourselves from experiencing the actual as actual?[19]

How long, indeed? One might answer: Until we have
recovered the perspective that the spectacular advances
in knowledge of recent generations have served to be-
cloud. Until we have become aware that the poetic eye
is capable of seeing as deeply into nature and man as the
scientific eye. Because poetry is "innocent" in not making
demands on us—in "letting us be," to use a favorite
Heideggerian phrase—we have been looking elsewhere,
inquiring after truth in the more practical and theoretical
realms, the more actionable kinds of knowledge. The
sciences can never let us alone as poetry, and the arts in
general, always do. Hence it is easily possible for us to
"see" a primrose as simply a yellow primrose, a Lake
Constance as merely a body of water. Seen this way
poetry and imagination are embellishments on the actual.
They simply adorn that which only the exact sciences
can describe and detail.

Some of us find the greatest promise of the existentialist movement in this attempt to recover for thought the
insights and visions of artists. Precisely because philosophers like Heidegger are not approaching literature with
the usual queries and concerns of aesthetics, there is hope
that philosophers may once again take seriously the discoveries of creative writers who are not consciously seeking to "do" philosophy. Lately we have been so occupied
with the much-touted "two cultures" that we have paid
scant attention to a more serious estrangement, that between poets and thinkers, philosophy and literature.
Even those not interested in existentialism might well
grant, for instance, that real advances lately in ethics
are more likely discoverable in the writings of Dostoevsky

19. *Existence and Being*, p. 275.

or Camus than in most academic moralists. Perhaps something of the same may be said for certain other traditional disciplines of philosophy. At least I find Heidegger's investigation of poetic works highly suggestive in this regard.

At the same time an important caveat is very much to the point. Poetry may be the most innocent of occupations, as Hölderlin has told us, but language, the poet's medium, is "the most dangerous of possessions," as he has also reminded us in the same poem. One senses that the older Heidegger is becoming less and less critical of poetic utterances, less inclined to apply the same standards of phenomenological analysis to the art work that he applies to the history of thought. Heidegger has a deeply religious nature, though it is surely not Christian in any specific sense. There is a danger in his fascination with language, in the almost irresistible impulse to play with it which sometimes tends to divert him from his task. Though this is a very innocent occupation, it is not less dangerous for that reason.

We notice a similar tendency in Plato, but one of which Plato was fully aware. Precisely because he loved poetry so much, he was on guard against its seductions. In the *Metaphysics* Aristotle repeats what he calls a Greek proverb: "Bards tell many a lie."[20] And Plato in the *Republic* speaks of the ancient quarrel between philosophy and poetry and bids us be on our guard against the enticements of the poets.[21] This ancient quarrel he, of course, detected as a quarrel within himself. While loving them, he distrusted poets and poetry because they were unable to distinguish truth from error in their gnomic utterances. One would like to see something of this same distrust in Heidegger, a heightened awareness

20. Aristotle, *Metaphysics*, 983a.
21. Plato, *Republic*, Book 10, 607c *et passim*.

that poets can lead us astray as well as lead us to truth.

Hölderlin's famous line begins with: "Full of merit, yet poetically, man dwells. . . ." Heidegger tends to neglect this opening phrase, *Voll Verdienst,* and to interpret only the part: "poetically man dwells on this earth." In the one place where he does take up the "full of merit" phrase, he makes it qualify the adverb "poetically." Hölderlin is not, according to Heidegger, contrasting "full of merit" with "poetically" or subordinating the latter to the former. Rather it is the other way around. The poet's "yet" means something like "to be sure."[22] He recognizes that Hölderlin means by "full of merit" man's civilizing capacities, such as building, planting, holding societies together by practical and political activities. But Heidegger tries to suggest that such prosaic activities are also poetical in Hölderlin's vision, that building and planting and the workaday world are poetical in essence.

Perhaps I can put this cautionary criticism of Heidegger's enterprise best by disagreement with this interpretation of his. I do not, of course, know what Hölderlin really intended by these cryptic lines. But I do believe that man should dwell prosaically on earth as well as poetically. He must first build a house in a very literal sense in order to dwell in it poetically as a home. Where there is no vision the people perish, as one of the proverbs in the Bible reminds us. But they will perish just as infallibly unless there is a kind of care-taking that centers on the prosaic functions of existence. Poetry can tempt a man to forget that he has a calling to provide the utilitarian means for imaginative "dwelling," by being first of all concerned with the material conditions of existence in the sense of man's moral and social well-being.

It was Albert Hofstadter who recently pointed out in a

22. *Vorträge und Aufsätze,* p. 191.

brilliant article[23] that Heidegger's conception of truth as "unconcealment and lighting" leads him to forget that the concept of truth has long had a relevance and meaning in the ethical sphere as well. Truth means right as well as radiance. And Hofstadter suggests that this stress on light and radiance may well be a reason for the comparative absence of the ethical emphasis in Heidegger's thought. One should add that it was just this attentiveness to the ethical good which led Plato to reluctant criticism of poets and poetry.

In saying this I do not wish to be understood as criticizing Heidegger for placing primary emphasis on the power of imagination and poetry. Man is not first a prosaic being and then in his leisure able to live poetically. The prose of life is primary not in this Philistine sense that labor is more elemental and real to him than poetizing. That we tend to think so in advanced civilizations testifies, in my opinion, to a fundamental derangement in our true relations to our fellows and to the earth and sky. In this I agree with Heidegger. But I intend my criticism in a different sense. Man's first vocation is that of taking care of himself and his fellows in a moral and social way, and this, though not divorced from poetry, is frequently a prosaic task. Like Plato's cave dweller who escaped from the cave, it is necessary for men to return and take up the task of education, even though by preference they would live in the sun's rays. Man's first task, I think, is justice, and if we can make no conclusive progress on it without imagination, poetry alone is not enough. Poetry has a seductive power, as the Greeks understood far better than most of us do, and it must be controlled in the interests of the pursuit of the good.

The notion of morality in our specialist age is usually

23. "Truth of Being," *The Journal of Philosophy*, vol. 62, no. 7 (April 1, 1965).

given a too limited scope. But it does mean something more concrete than providing man with a love of the beautiful and the true in the sense of a vision of what is. It means also providing a sense for the political in the ancient and honorable meaning of that term as well as a capacity for friendship in the private sphere of life. *Physis* and *logos* may be more ultimate problems than are *politeia* and *philia,* but some of us believe that the latter are primary for mortals. In this respect Hölderlin's lines seem to put first things first, contrary to Heidegger's interpretation, in noting that men dwell "full of merit," and *yet* "poetically on this earth."

In affirming Heidegger's emphasis on the sameness of goal of poets and thinkers, I shall conclude with the hope that when philosophy discovers poetry it will not abandon the critical intelligence with which we are slowly learning to approach the deliverances of science.